CRACKING THE
Value
Code

Based on a three-year, 10,000 - company study

CRACKING THE
Value
Code

How successful businesses are
creating wealth in the New Economy

By
Richard E.S. Boulton
Barry D. Libert
Steve M. Samek

HarperBusiness
An Imprint of HarperCollins*Publishers*

HarperCollins books may be purchased for educational, business, or sales promotional use. For information, please write: Special Markets Department, HarperCollins Publishers Inc., 10 East 53rd Street, New York, NY 10022.

Book design by Ken Silvia Design, illustration of figures and page layout by Bruce Sanders Design & Illustration.

Library of Congress Cataloging-in-Publication Data has been applied for.

ISBN 0-06-662063-5

00 01 02 03 04 10 9 8 7 6 5 4 3 2 1

For Fiona, Honor, and Fraser
with my love.
—RB

To my sons, who taught me how to CARE,
and to my wife, who taught me how to love.
—BL

For my parents,
who cracked the code
of instilling values.
Thank you.
—SS

Contents

ACKNOWLEDGMENTS

Like any book, this one was a collaborative effort involving many people. In particular, this book would not have been possible without the unwavering commitment of two people.

Ed Giniat, managing partner of Arthur Andersen's Healthcare Practice, invested endless energy and insight in this initiative from the earliest years. He truly was a fourth author.

And Ellen Wolfe worked tirelessly during the past four years to shape and articulate many of the ideas presented in the manuscript, while continuing to remind us that "what is intangible is most enduring."

We gained much from the wisdom of Arthur Andersen experts, including: Jeannot Blanchet, Gregory Jonas, and Sridhar Ramamoorti (professional standards and reporting); Robert Hiebeler (best practices and business processes); James DeLoach (risk management); Carl Waller and Mark Miller (performance measurement); Tom Frederick (eBusiness); and Joel Hagan (the New Economy). A special thank you goes to Robert Hodgkinson for his wide-ranging intellectual contributions, including his insights into the role of information in the New Economy.

We are grateful to Tony Grimsditch, Madhu Nott, Andrew North, and Graham Atkinson for their significant contributions to the research and development of the concepts presented in these pages.

We thank Donna Sammons Carpenter, Maurice Coyle, Ruth Hlavacek, Toni Porcelli, Helen Rees, Cindy Sammons, John Sammons, and Robert W. Stock of Wordworks, Inc., who were important to the birth and life of this project. And we also are grateful to Ken Silvia, who designed the book, and to Bruce Sanders, Robin Cheung and Matthew Harless for illustration and page layout support.

We acknowledge the many distinguished people who started and contributed to the dialogue about value creation over the past decade. We were influenced especially by Michael Hammer's and James Champy's writing on business processes; Christopher A. Bartlett's and Sumantra Ghoshal's work on people, purpose, and processes; Frederick F. Reichheld and the Forum Corporation on customers; Karl Erik Sveiby on knowledge; Thomas A. Stewart on the broader field of intellectual capital; Baruch Lev on intangibles; David Teece on a resource-based view of strategy; and the broad contributions to thinking on strategy by Peter Drucker, Gary Hamel, C. K. Prahalad, Charles Handy, and Michael Porter.

We are indebted to our publisher, HarperCollins, especially to Adrian Zackheim, and Lisa Berkowitz, as well as our entire marketing team—Lynn Goldberg, Barbara Henricks, Mike Hatcliffe, and Jane Ostrander. From our first conversations with each of them and their subsequent reading of the manuscript, they encouraged our efforts to "crack the code"—to unravel the question of value creation in our time.

Finally, we must thank our clients, whose intangible assets in the form of knowledge and relationships greatly enriched our learning process as we sought to understand how organizations are creating and realizing value in the New Economy.

INTRODUCTION
What is Value?

"The real voyage of discovery consists . . . in seeing with new eyes."

—Marcel Proust[1]

Q. How much does the New Economy weigh?

Answer: A lot less than you might think. U.S. Federal Reserve Chairman Alan Greenspan posed that question in a speech in Dallas, Texas. His conclusion: The country's economy is proportionally lighter, in a literal sense, than at any time in this half-century.[2]

By conventional measures, he noted, the U.S. gross domestic product is five times what it was 50 years ago, but its physical weight has grown only slightly. That is because the smokestack industries of the past produced tangible goods. Today, a significant part of the country's economic output is intangible, and that part is growing at exponential rates.

A newspaper available on-line in digital form, for example, weighs nothing compared with the physical product, and it can be transported via the Internet at a cost of next to nothing. A software program weighs no more than a few ounces. Music is no longer weighted down by packaging at all, as listeners download it from the Internet into their computers or MP-3 players.

Greenspan put it succinctly when he said that "virtually unimaginable a half-century ago was the extent to which concepts and ideas would substitute for physical resources and human brawn in the production of goods and services."

What does all of this mean for you and your organization? It means that the New Economy is not just hype and high-flying stocks, that it represents a new reality that no company can afford to ignore. It means that you and your business are going to have to embrace a new model of how to create value.

Why? Because today's economy—built as it is on a foundation of new technologies, globalization, a new generation of people entering the workplace, and the increased importance of intangible assets—is different from anything any of us have encountered before.

In the words of *Fast Company* magazine, "a global revolution is changing business, and that business is changing the world. New rules of business, and a new breed of company [that] will challenge the corporate status quo. No part of business will be immune. The structure of the company is changing; relationships between companies are changing; the nature of work is changing; and the definition of success is changing. The result will be a new world order representing unparalleled opportunity and unprecedented uncertainty." [3]

Organizations are creating value in totally new ways, using assets and combinations of assets heretofore unrecognized under traditional accounting systems—and certainly unmeasured. The realization of the enormous economic value of people, for instance, has sparked a no-holds-barred war for talent, often at the expense of traditional attitudes about work itself and old ways of recognizing and rewarding employees. In such a milieu, old methods of managing and measuring are simply not up to the task.

To ignore the significance of the changes afoot in business today is to ignore reality itself as the page turns on a new millennium. And what organization can thrive, or even survive, in a world of illusion? None.

Those changes are manifest in every day's headlines: When it turns out, for example, that almost every new member of the *Forbes* list of 400 wealthiest individuals in 1999 built his or her fortune on technology; when an upstart Internet company like America Online, Inc., could seek to acquire the Time Warner, Inc. media empire; when Microsoft Corporation achieved a market value exceeding the combined value of eight giant U.S. corporations (Boeing, Caterpillar, Ford, General Motors, Kellogg, Eastman Kodak Company, J.P. Morgan & Company and Sears, Roebuck). As the millennium began, Microsoft's market value stood at $602.4 billion—built almost entirely on intangibles.

This book examines how successful businesses like these are creating value in the New Economy. And we draw a key distinction between value creation and value realization. Value creation—that is, future value captured in the form of increased market capitalization—is how successful businesses are creating value in the New Economy. Value realization—that is, value captured in the form of past and current earnings or cash flows—is what underlies both traditional accounting and most of today's management information systems (including EVA). It necessarily means that many organizations take a short-term view, ignoring the drivers of value creation today, especially intangible assets.

In the pages that follow, you will find a new set of tools that we have developed to help you create value in the New Economy. It is called Value Dynamics, and it is based, in part, on an intensive three-year, 10,000-company research project by professionals at Arthur Andersen. It speaks directly to the four realities of the New Economy.

! New business models are emerging.

Businesses are their assets, all of their assets—tangible and intangible, owned and unowned. But in the New Economy, it is intangible assets such as relationships, knowledge, people, brands, and systems that are taking center stage. We see this in the new strategies and business models being developed by such powerhouses as Microsoft Corporation, E*TRADE Group, Inc., and Amazon.com, Inc. Successful companies will combine both old and New Economy assets. In fact, it is the combination and interaction of various assets—more than any other factor—that will determine a business' economic success.

! New business models create new risks.

Companies are increasingly employing unique business models, which push the boundaries of traditional controls. That is, leading-edge companies are finding that their management and measurement systems are no longer aligned with the assets that they are using to create value. What's more, the New Economy is producing a whole set of different risks—from new transactions and new markets to new technologies, new competitors, and new relationships. But risk in the New Economy encompasses the upside, as well as the downside. As a result, companies need to embrace (as well as manage) risk to prosper and succeed.

! New processes and tools are needed to succeed.

How a company builds and manages its portfolio of assets ultimately determines its success. But despite the growing importance of intangible assets in the New Economy, most businesses don't have formal processes and systems to manage these assets and the risks they create. And while some processes are becoming out-moded, others, from brand management to distance learning, are rising to importance. Businesses need new processes for setting strategy, operating, managing risk, and using information in decision making.

! Transparency of information is vital to value creation.

Even as new markets and technologies like the Internet create and distribute better information about all the assets that matter, managers need more to support value creation. Real-time financial reporting is almost a reality for some companies, as are systems integrating internal and external data for delivery to the corporate desktop.

Thus, businesses must recognize that the old models of information for decision-making—including measurement and reporting—are becoming obsolete. Under the models of the past, companies have focused primarily on internal information, while resisting disclosing more than the bare minimum required by regulation. The model of the future is transparent and user-driven, and allows stakeholders to readily access the information they need to know, when they need to know it. Companies will need to measure all of their value-creating assets, including the difficult-to-measure intangibles. Being approximately right is more important in these areas than being precisely wrong.

With these issues as a backdrop, you are about to begin a journey with a single destination—value creation. What to do differently and how to do it are the subjects of this book.

In the New Economy, managers must think of competition in terms of competing business models, whose power comes in part from how the assets within their portfolios interact. Specifically, we argue that assets —including technologies—combine, re-combine, and interact in infinite ways to create economic value. Using human genetics as an analogy, we think of assets as the substance of the "business genome," the economic DNA of enterprises.

Scientists have identified the four amino acids that make up DNA and the double-helix structure of the molecule itself.   Different sequences of these four bases generate the infinite variety of biological life on the planet, as well as the genetic messages that help create the individuality of every human being. Based on these discoveries, scientists are in a race to map the human genome. Their goal: Crack the biochemical code for each of the 100,000 genes that determine the physical characteristics of the human body.

Similarly, companies in today's superheated economies are in a race to discover the underlying code of value creation. That is, they are trying

The interaction of a company's assets— its economic DNA—creates or destroys value.

to find out which combinations of assets—tangible and intangible—create the greatest amounts of economic value and to avoid those combinations that destroy it.

In biological dynamics, says Brian Goodwin, a British biologist, "what is important is the pattern of relationships and interactions that exist and how they contribute to the system as an integrated whole."[4] So too with the dynamics of value creation. It is the complex interaction of a company's mix of assets—its economic DNA if you will—that creates or destroys value.

In this book, we show how you can begin to crack the value code for your company. Our insights come not only from the three-year Arthur Andersen study, but also from our own work with clients. They reflect our experience as consultants to companies in every industry and on every continent.

To bring our ideas alive, we offer a wealth of company case studies. We sincerely hope that you will ask yourself how the insights of Value Dynamics can be applied to your own organization. Look for the questions to answer at the end of each chapter. These will help you frame your ideas in terms of the value creation journey for your company.

Specifically, here's what lies ahead.

- **Part I** opens with a question: How do companies create value today? Our answer: To succeed, they need to see what matters—all of the assets contributing to value creation.

- **Part II** shows how a number of businesses in different industries are leading the way by leveraging specific types of assets to create exceptional value.

- **Part III** outlines the challenges you face—and the actions you need to take—to design, build, and manage a business model for success in the New Economy. Look for tools to help you examine your own company.

Finally, the Epilogue looks to the future. It encourages business leaders, investors, employees, customers, regulators, and professional associations to take up the effort to better understand how business and society can thrive.

▶ What's next?

The focus throughout this book is on value creation—seeing, investing in, managing, and measuring all of what matters in the New Economy. The goal—to crack the code of value creation.

What stops companies from participating in unprecedented value-creating opportunities? The first chapter uncovers the problem.

See What Matters

1

How Are Businesses Creating Value in the New Economy?

"The first sign we don't know what we are doing is an obsession with numbers."

—Johann Wolfgang von Goethe

H ere is what we might call a number problem. Say you are interested in new media stocks. The year is 1993, and you come across an upstart Internet company—for the moment, let's call it XYZ Corporation.

It is based in Dulles, Virginia, and has just 124 employees. It has net income of $4.3 million from annual revenues of $31.6 million. Its market capitalization? A mere $168 million.

Few people pay any attention to XYZ—and no wonder. "Nothing grows under big trees," someone once said. XYZ is in the shade of some giant trees, any of which has the resources to easily oust XYZ from its precarious perch. One of those trees is a company we'll call ABC Corporation.

ABC is a New York-based multi-media giant with revenues of $13.1 billion, net income of $86 million a year, and a market capitalization of $10.9 billion.

So there you are, back in 1993, and the question before you is this: Which company are you going to invest in? The right pick—as you probably have guessed—would have been XYZ, better known as America Online, Inc.[1]

By the beginning of the year 2000, seven years later, AOL had grown into the world's premier on-line server, with a market value of $169.6 billion. It made a profit of $1 billion in 1999 on revenues of $5.7 billion.

Meanwhile, ABC, otherwise known as Time Warner, Inc., the big tree whose shade failed to stunt AOL's growth, had a market cap of $93 billion on January 1, 2000.[2] Revenues at the end of the third quarter of 1999 were $23.5 billion with net income at $1.2 billion.

If you had invested $1,000 in AOL at the opening of trading in January, 1993, it would have grown to a hefty $332,057 by year-end 1999. Meanwhile, the same amount invested in Time Warner—a company at that time with almost 500 times the sales of AOL and 24 times the net income—would be worth $4,944.

This means that when, just 10 days into the new millennium, AOL and Time Warner announced their intention to merge, AOL was destined to be the dominant partner in the huge new company.[3]

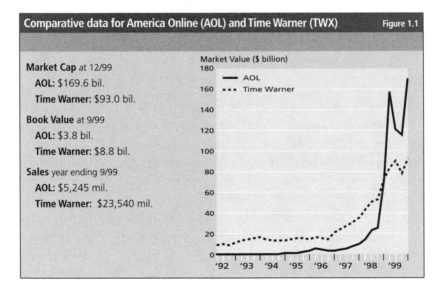

Comparative data for America Online (AOL) and Time Warner (TWX)   Figure 1.1

Market Cap at 12/99
AOL: $169.6 bil.
Time Warner: $93.0 bil.

Book Value at 9/99
AOL: $3.8 bil.
Time Warner: $8.8 bil.

Sales year ending 9/99
AOL: $5,245 mil.
Time Warner: $23,540 mil.

Next question: How could you have been prescient enough back in 1993 to choose little America Online over the powerhouse called Time Warner? What could you have known about AOL that might have clued you in on where to put your money?

You might have invested in the company from the beginning if you had identified and understood the value of all the assets that made up its business—not just the bricks and mortar and the financial assets represented on the balance sheet, but the intangible assets that traditional accounting pretty much ignores.

In that case, you might have known about an intangible asset by the name of Stephen M. Case, who, together with the company's president and chief operating officer, Robert W. Pittman, devised the business model that would define and dominate the fledgling on-line industry. You might have understood his intention to create extraordinary wealth on the back of another intangible AOL asset, its small, but uncommonly loyal, customer base—now grown to more than 22 million subscribers.

As *The New York Times* put it following the merger, "Mr. Case worked for 15 years, through obscurity and ridicule, to achieve his vision that chatting on a computer screen would become as important a communications medium as the telephone or television."

But how could you have known from the start about Steve Case and the genius of his vision? Who or what could have pointed you to AOL as a company that would introduce radically new ways of doing business in the years ahead?

You certainly would not have found the key in books on management, or in strategic-planning manuals, or even in *The Wall Street Journal.* Nor would you have found all the information you needed about AOL's value-creating potential on its balance sheet. You still won't, for that matter.

Leadership, one of the key factors in determining the future prospects of a company, is invisible on its balance sheet. So are many of the other assets that are essential to the creation of value in the New Economy. In fact, for an organization to succeed today and in the years ahead, it is going to have to create value in totally different ways, using assets that are not even captured by our current accounting systems.

The advent of the New Economy has made a new approach to value creation mandatory. Today's business world has been transformed by globalization, breakthrough technologies, and new levels of competition in which old rules of business are constantly breached. These are the hallmarks of the New Economy, and they leave companies with no choice but to develop new business models attuned to the new reality. Old ways of managing and measuring assets no longer suffice.

This book is intended to be a guide to creating value in the New Economy. It points to the innovative strategies and processes that leading organizations have adopted to make the most of their assets. And it provides a tool—the Value Dynamics Framework—to help managers exploit all their assets.

As it stands, companies give short shrift to a whole range of assets that don't appear on the balance sheet, which is dominated by physical and financial assets. Value Dynamics adds three more categories of assets that are driving wealth creation in the New Economy: Employee and supplier assets, customer assets, and organization assets. As you will see in later chapters, the Value Dynamics Framework also lists the individual assets within each category. Just as scientists are breaking the code of life with their discovery of DNA, so the companies we describe here are starting to identify the building blocks of economic value—or, as our book title puts it, they are *Cracking the Value Code*.

AOL isn't the only company that has pioneered new ways of creating value today. Another is the Dell Computer Corporation.[4]

Back in the late 1980s, Dell, based in the Austin, Texas, suburb of Round Rock, laid the groundwork for huge success by adopting its "Be Direct" business model. It called for the company to serve customers directly over toll-free phone lines. Only after a personal computer was sold were the parts for that machine ordered. The "direct" model eliminated dealers and inventories as well, and passed the savings on to Dell customers.

As a result, the company was able to seize a hefty share of the market for personal computers—for a while at least. Then its rivals in computer manufacturing cloned key parts of the Dell model, and its market share began to drop.

But Dell found another way to out-innovate its competitors. It reinvented itself as the hub of a system of suppliers intimately linked by long-term contracts and information networks. And it took advantage

Companies, like Dell and The Gap, are cracking the code of value with new business models.

of new technology to establish a strong presence on the World Wide Web. So successful are Dell's Web-based sales and customer service operations that they now account for almost 30 percent of its new business. The company has no traditional distribution network standing between itself and its customers.

These days, a Dell customer may be served by a telephone or on-line order taker who actually works for Matrix Marketing, a division of

Cincinnati Bell, Inc. (Cincinnati, Ohio). The Matrix employee hands the order to a coordinator who actually works for Roadway Express, Inc. (Akron, Ohio). The coordinator, in turn, may pass the order along to the Dell factory in Austin, Texas, Limerick, Ireland, or Panang, Malaysia. Meanwhile, Roadway directs parts suppliers such as Selectron, which furnishes motherboards, and Maxtor, which makes hard drives, to replenish stocks in Austin, Limerick, or Panang. And it tells United Parcel Service of America, Inc. (Atlanta, Georgia), to ship the finished computer to the Dell customer.

But here is our question: How does Dell Computer create value for itself and its investors? When it relies on outsiders to handle so many aspects of its operations, what does the company actually do?

Answer: Dell makes the most of its suppliers. That means that its future depends to a great extent upon its skill in selecting and managing other people's organizations—an intangible asset that is not exactly a line item on an income statement or balance sheet. Has doing less of the work itself hurt Dell? Hardly. The company, which maintains offices in 32 countries, is a nonstop money-making machine. Its sales for the year ending October 1999 reached $23.6 billion—up 41 percent from the previous year. Net income climbed by 25 percent to $1.7 billion. Among *Fortune* magazine's "100 Fastest Growing Companies" for that year, Dell was the leader in return on stockholders' equity with a three-year annual return on investment of 186 percent.[5]

Of course, Dell's competitors have not stood still. Its chief rival, Compaq Computer Corporation, is now in the midst of a major reorganization, and is repositioning itself with new management at the helm. But Dell still prevails in the stock market. Its market capitalization at year-end 1999 was $130.8 billion, nearly three times that of Compaq.

Another question: How does the giant clothing retailer Gap Inc. create value?[6] It's obvious, you say?

Gap Inc., based in San Francisco, California, is a fast-growing retailer, the biggest in the United States, with more than 2,900 stores, 110,000 employees, and sales of some $10.8 billion through October, 1999. And it creates value with its unpretentious, comfortable clothes.

But The Gap is also a way of doing business. Virtually every aspect of its operations is dictated from headquarters. That includes the design of its stores, the design and presentation of its clothes, the attire of its salespeople, the hours it is open, even the bodyforms it uses.

But if you ask Millard S. "Mickey" Drexler, president and chief executive officer, to define his company, you are likely to get a different answer. He asks why a clothing store can't be more like other global brands, such as AOL and Disney. "We are limited," he once declared, "only by our imagination."

You won't find many brands like AOL and Disney in the clothing business, one of the most mature around. Usually, fashion houses streak across the firmament on the inspiration of a single creative mind, then fizzle. Drexler thinks his company can be an exception. He sees it as a stable planet in the brand firmament, and he is well on the way to making it so.

Here is the thing about brands: They must be of a dependable and consistent quality. The Gap is surely that. "Growth without quality," Drexler likes to say, "is nothing more than a shortcut to failure."

Brands must also be accessible, and new Gap outlets are popping up everywhere. In the first 10 months of 1999, Gap Inc. opened 380 stores, a 20 percent increase in the number of outlets over the previous year. Brands must be in the public eye—promoted incessantly through

Drexler views the company as a "portfolio" of brands limited "only by our imagination."

advertisements, on the Internet, through the buzz. The Gap spent about 4.4 percent of its sales on advertising in 1998, up from 1.7 percent of sales in 1997.

Clearly, the company has made the scene.

Drexler views the company these days as a "portfolio of brands." He has been busily leveraging the original Gap brand by adding line extensions. Among them: Gapkids, babyGap, and GapScents. His most recent addition is GapBody, shops that sell everything from candles to boxer shorts.

Drexler is onto something. By year-end 1999, The Gap had a market value of $39.1 billion. During the past decade, Gap Inc.'s annual return to investors has averaged 38.8 percent. That is better than Coca-Cola's record of 35.3 percent, the Gillette Company's 29.4 percent, and Disney's 21.6 percent.

Back to our question: How does Gap Inc. create value? Answer: The company is exploiting its portfolio of brands, an intangible asset, to generate new value for its customers and wealth for its investors and other stakeholders. But it isn't getting much help in managing its brand from traditional management, measurement, or reporting systems. Brands, you see, don't show up on the balance sheet.

Our last and most important question: How do you create value in the New Economy? The answer, as our examples suggest, is more profound and more complex than you might suspect. That is why we have

The assets hidden below the surface of financial statements drive stock prices.

written this book. Today, more than ever, the question of how to create value occupies the waking hours of the world's business leaders, investors, academic researchers, and economists, all of whom recognize that the old answers no longer work.

In the pages that follow, we offer a new way of thinking about value—and new ways of creating value in the new millennium. We propose a fundamental shift in the way business is done, as well as in the management theories and practices that support it. We start with the most basic of questions: What's a business, anyway? And we reply: A business is its assets—all of its assets.

These assets are tangible and intangible, measured and unmeasured, owned and unowned. And even though not all of them appear on a company's balance sheet, they drive business success in the New Economy.

Businesses assemble their assets in combinations specific to them. That is, they use their assets to build unique business models.

It is the business model that ultimately determines whether an organization creates or destroys value and in what ways. Or, in our parlance, business models determine whether a company actually succeeds in cracking the value code.

Traditional economics saw wealth flowing primarily from an organization's land, capital, labor, and entrepreneurship. Land, and then capital, were seen as the scarcest resources. Labor was the abundant brute force used by owners of land and capital to exploit their resources, rather than a source of knowledge and innovation.

It is clear that this formulation fails to encompass all the sources of wealth in today's business environment. We believe, and offer evidence to show, that traditional approaches to management and measurement are no longer adequate. Change now comes too fast and from too many directions.

In this book, we seek to answer questions that confront all of us in the New Economy: How do we create value for our organizations? What new strategies and capabilities are required for us to create value and manage risk? What assets are most important in the New Economy?

When a company like Dell, for example, outsources almost everything from sales to manufacturing to research and development, its drivers of long-term value creation can hardly be judged simply in terms of traditional tangible assets. Intangible assets count heavily. The quality of its supplier relationships and managerial know-how, for example, are critical. So are its customer relationships and the channels (especially the Internet) that it uses to communicate with those customers.

Where do we find evidence of how value is created in the New Economy? The financial markets. Investors have increasingly come to understand that it is often the assets hidden below the surface of financial statements that drive stock prices.

That isn't to say that investors—especially professional ones—no longer value companies based on current and future cash flows. They still use that yardstick, but with a difference. Today, investors take a broader view of what is driving cash flows, including non-balance sheet assets and the ways a company exploits them. Lacking consistent ways to categorize and accurately measure the intangible drivers of value, many investors are forced to rely on what amounts to little more than informed guesswork.

One dramatic symptom of the changes in the way the equity markets value companies is the growing discrepancy between market capitalization and book value. Another is the preference of investors for New Economy companies and industries, especially those that are leading the way in exploiting the power and potential of the Internet.

Consider these statistics: $100 invested in real estate in 1982 was worth at the beginning of the year 2000 a little more than $375. The same $100 would have produced more than three times that amount (or $1,280) if invested in the Dow Jones Industrial Average, and nearly 85 times that amount (or $31,706) if invested in software stocks.[7]

Book value and market value remained relatively similar in the United States for many years, even though these two values are derived in altogether different ways.[8] Indeed, their long-standing parity contributed to the widespread misunderstanding of what the balance sheet represents.

In recent years, however, the gap between book and market value, which first opened in the 1980s, has turned into a chasm. On average, the book value of publicly traded U.S. companies was 28 percent of market value by 1998.

To illustrate this point further, let's look at the relationship between market and book value for several companies in different industries.

- At the end of the third quarter 1999, AOL's book value was a miniscule 3.3 percent of its total market capitalization. In other words nearly 97 percent of AOL's value was not to be found on the balance sheet.

- The Coca-Cola Company's book value was at 7.9 percent of its total market value, while PepsiCo, Inc.'s was at 15.5 percent.

- Organizations that rely more heavily on physical assets may have quite different market-to-book ratios. For example, the book value of Borders, the national chain bookstore, was almost 70 percent of its market value. The financial services giant, Merrill Lynch & Co. Inc., had a book-to-market ratio of 49 percent.

Even though book value and market value serve different purposes, the gap between them is instructive. Investors are clearly leading the way in trying to understand how value is created. Now, management, measurement, and reporting systems must catch up.

Scholars have devoted increasing attention in recent years to the relationship between stock prices, on the one hand, and earnings and book values, on the other. They have asked whether the relevance of the two accounting measures has declined, particularly for companies with large investments in intangible assets. Some academics maintain that earnings and book value still had a strong impact on market value in the years between 1953 and 1993. Others give them much less importance.[9]

Though experts may disagree as to degree, it is abundantly clear that companies are increasingly using new assets to create value. Baruch Lev, Director of the Vincent C. Ross Institute for Accounting Research and the Project for Research on Intangibles, Stern School of Business at New York University, describes it by saying, "In the past several decades, there has been a dramatic shift, a transformation, in what economists call the production functions of companies—the major assets that create value and growth. Intangibles are fast becoming substitutes for physical assets. At the same time, there has been complete stagnation in our measurement and reporting systems. I'm not talking only about financial reports and Internet investments, but also internal measurements—accounting and reporting inside companies." [10]

These issues—and the debate surrounding them—motivated us to

> **Has the relevance of some accounting measures declined in today's world, particularly for companies with large investments in intangible assets? Questions like this motivated us to undertake research into value creation.**

undertake a major research project on value creation. And with stock market trends strongly suggesting the emergence of a new value-creation model, we turned first to the financial markets in an effort to crack the value code of the New Economy.

Using a database containing the more than 10,000 businesses actively traded on stock markets in the United States, as well as data that identified some 450 financial and nonfinancial variables over the past two decades, we analyzed patterns of value creation.[11]

We sought to answer a number of key questions. Among them were the following.

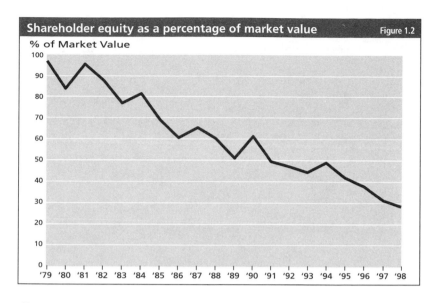

Shareholder equity as a percentage of market value   Figure 1.2

How are companies creating value?

Intangible assets play an increasing role in creating value for companies. Between 1978 and 1998, the non-book value of all companies rose from 5 percent to 72 percent of market value, as figure 1.2 shows. (A reminder: We define non-book value as market value minus book value.) In other words, book value declined from 95 percent of market value to 28 percent during that twenty-year period. This trend, if anything, is accelerating.

In addition, companies with more physical assets used capital less efficiently. (See Figure 1.3.) The top 20 percent of companies, based on five-year shareholder returns, generated returns more than 500 percent greater than those of the bottom 20 percent of companies. And those bottom 20 percent of shareholder return performers consumed, on average, 20 times more fixed assets per unit of revenue than did the top performers.

Which industries and companies are creating the most value?

A minority of companies create a disproportionate share of value in the New Economy. Fully 71 percent of the publicly traded companies we

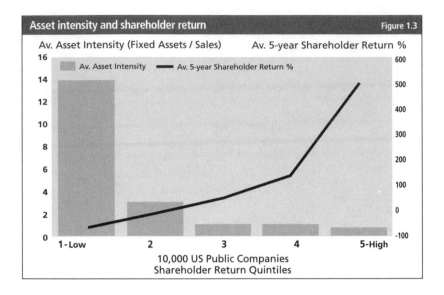

Asset intensity and shareholder return   Figure 1.3

Av. Asset Intensity (Fixed Assets / Sales)   Av. 5-year Shareholder Return %

10,000 US Public Companies
Shareholder Return Quintiles

examined had below-average shareholder returns over a research span from 1978 to 1996. Twenty-nine percent generated most of the value and raised the average for all.

In addition, to identify the characteristics of efficient value-creation companies, we ranked organizations by market capitalization divided by net sales.[12] (See Figure 1.4.) The most highly valued companies per unit of revenue also had the highest ratio of market-to-book. In addition, the top 10 percent of companies had an average market-to-book ratio approximately double that of the second 10 percent, and four times that of the bottom 10 percent. In other words, the companies in this top decile were dramatically and disproportionately more efficient at leveraging assets that were not on their books.

We also identified the industries in which these highly-valued companies were most heavily represented. They were disproportionately to be found in four industries—high technology, health care, communications, and financial services.

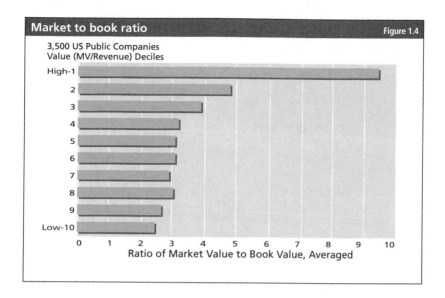

Market to book ratio   Figure 1.4

3,500 US Public Companies
Value (MV/Revenue) Deciles

Ratio of Market Value to Book Value, Averaged

Which companies produce the best ratios of risk and return?

Risk, as measured by historic stock volatility, has been increasing for all industries, with the range of volatilities approximately doubling in the period from 1981 to 1997. (See Figure 1.5.) Organizations with fewer physical assets—that is, low physical-asset intensity—fared better. They produced increasing returns without a commensurate increase in volatility compared with companies that had more physical assets (high physical-asset intensity). And the corollary was also true: Organizations with the most physical assets had the worst ratios of return and volatility.

How are corporate leaders responding to these changes?

We surveyed more than 250 executives across a wide industry spectrum about issues related to value creation. Some 85 percent of these executives reported that they recognized the importance of investment in intangible assets like employees and customers. However, less than 35 percent said that they acted accordingly.[13]

Although chief executive officers ranked "customer satisfaction" and

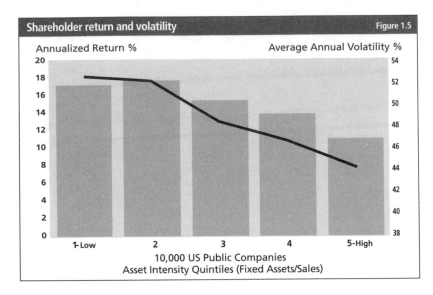

Shareholder return and volatility   Figure 1.5

Annualized Return %   Average Annual Volatility %

10,000 US Public Companies
Asset Intensity Quintiles (Fixed Assets/Sales)

"employee retention" as the top two measurements of value creation, neither is included in today's formal reporting systems. (See Figure 1.6.) A majority acknowledged the need to measure more of the key factors for success in the New Economy, but they blamed unsatisfactory measurement systems, previous failed attempts, and current costs for keeping them from doing so.

Our research supported what is increasingly recognized: Much of the value being created today falls outside the formal financial reporting systems. Consider Microsoft's market and book value. Microsoft became the world's most highly valued company in 1998. By January 1, 2000, its market value had climbed to some $600 billion. That's the value perceived by investors, even though the company's book assets were only $31.3 billion at the end of the third quarter 1999.[14]

Back to the core question of this chapter: How are companies creating value as we turn the page on a new millennium? Specifically, how can you, as a manager, create greater value for your organization?

The answer is, by identifying your company's most important sources of value—paying close attention to intangible assets that fall largely outside the formal measurement system—and by building your strategies accordingly.

In the New Economy, sources of value include both traditional assets, such as financial capital and physical facilities, and entirely new classes of assets. Transactions promoted by new technologies and the Internet are building new markets and connecting people and compa-

Essential performance measures over the next 3 to 5 years — Figure 1.6

nies in more efficient ways that compress time and space. The result is improved productivity and asset use.

In that new environment, both corporate managers and investors taking risks with new business models need a better understanding of the true sources of value. The Value Dynamics approach can guide them to that goal. Regardless of whether the stock market goes up or down, and whether individual stocks fly high or low on any given day, our thesis stands. That's because our focus is on how long-term value is created. And in the New Economy, intangible assets and new technologies are key to winning in the marketplace.

▶ What's next?

The first step to value creation is to properly identify a company's sources of value—that is, its assets, all of them.

Correctly defining assets is one of the keys to cracking the value code. It is also the subject of the next chapter.

Ask Yourself:

- What are your company's most important assets — both tangible and intangible? Have these assets changed in the last few years? If so, how?

- How does your company invest in all its various assets? Does it have a framework or context for making these investment decisions?

- If you are a public company, what is your market capitalization? If you aren't public, how would the market value your organization?

- Has your company's market-to-book ratio changed over the last few years? In addition to physical and financial assets, what other assets contribute to its market value?

- How much does your company invest in intangible assets and new technologies? Is this enough given the increasing importance of intangibles and new technologies in the New Economy?

2

Businesses Are Their Assets— All Their Assets.

"Sometimes what counts can't be counted, and what can be counted doesn't count."

— Albert Einstein

W e have all seen the advertisements in which Peter Lynch, one-time investment star and current spokesman for Fidelity Investments, the Boston-based mutual-fund company, cautions viewers to "know what you own, and know why you own it."

Sound advice, certainly. But what, you may be wondering, does it have to do with running a business in the New Economy? What's it doing in a book about corporate value creation?[1]

On the face of it, the investment decisions made by corporate managers are quite different from those made by institutional and individual investors—but they have more in common than appears on first glance. Corporate managers, like investors, need to know just what assets their companies own and why they own them. And, like investors, they need to know what they paid for those assets and the return they produce. That's because assets—tangible and intangible, measured and unmeasured—are the building blocks of business value.

Generally speaking, managers know a great deal about their organizations' investments in physical and financial assets. What they often lack is information and insight about other sources of value—that is, their other assets.

Are we talking about obscure assets? Hardly.

To illustrate what we mean, try answering the following questions about assets your company relies on to create value:

- How many customers do you have? What do they buy from you and why? What do you spend to acquire and retain your customers? What is your customer turnover rate? Which ones won't be your customers next year?

- How many people does your company employ? What do you spend on them in the form of salary and benefits? What does your company spend to attract and retain them? What is your company's employee turnover? What does it cost to replace an experienced employee?

- Who are your key suppliers? What is your company's relationship with them? How well do they understand your business objectives? What does your company spend to attract and retain them? What does it cost to replace a supplier who knows your business?

- Who are your investors? How much do they invest in your company and why? Why do some choose to sell?

- What is unique about your systems and processes? How do they help you create value and manage risk? What opportunities do you have to codify and protect your intellectual assets?

- What is the value of your leadership team? How do you renew the value of these people?

- How do you invest in your corporate culture to support economic success?

These questions may appear simple at first glance, but they can be surprisingly difficult to answer. That's because they all focus on assets that fall outside the existing financial reporting system.

Neither is it easy to figure out how a company as a whole is affected by investing in one set of assets as opposed to another. So the truth is, many companies find it difficult indeed to know what assets they own and why.

Although sophisticated information systems have evolved to give companies a way to accumulate and manipulate large amounts of performance data, measurement still begins at a common source: the double-entry system of accounting.

First documented by a Franciscan friar and mathematician more than 500 years ago, the double-entry system was invented to give absentee owners an accounting of the money they provided to a venture or company.

Johann Wolfgang von Goethe, the noted 19th-century German writer and scientist, described double-entry bookkeeping as "one of the most beautiful discoveries of the human spirit," because it rests on a basic truth: Every economic event has two opposite and equal sides.

In practical terms, this means that to record a profit (or an increase in equity) of a particular amount, an organization must be able to point to either a new asset of equivalent size or to a liability that has disappeared. The same process applies in accounting for losses. Everything comes down to swapping assets for other assets, assets for liabilities, or liabilities for other liabilities—in other words, making assets, and liabilities go up or down by equivalent amounts.

Can a 500-year-old measurement system keep step with the New Economy?

Businesses use double-entry bookkeeping to record their own transactions. Equity grows or declines when there is a transaction to support that movement. If a company's inventory falls by $100,000, for example, and receivables go up by $150,000 because goods have been sold, equity increases by $50,000. The value of net assets and equity shown in the books is determined by transactions with third parties.

But what about transactions between owners of a business? What happens when owners, called investors, are providing the equity? When investors buy and sell stock in a company, these transactions create a problem. That's because they generate a value for equity that can be much different from what is shown in the books.

Historically, this happened only rarely. When more companies were privately owned and stock transactions more difficult, equity was determined by singular events caused by partnership changes or business acquisitions. When such transactions provided evidence that the equity of the business was worth more than the books showed, people inferred that a new asset had come to light. They called it goodwill.

Now fast-forward to the New Economy. Two things have changed. First, the 500-year-old accounting system reflects the value created or destroyed by transactions. But in the New Economy, value can be created or destroyed without any transactions with third parties, for example, the clinical approval of a new drug, or changes in regulations. And second, the equity of most significant businesses is now traded continuously on major stock exchanges. Companies rely less on debt financing and the equity held by long-term family members or local stockholders. The world's wealthier nations are producing a tsunami of investment in global financial markets, changing them forever.

A company's value is determined daily as millions of shareholders buy and sell its stock. Management, as a result, can see the value of the company as determined by third-party investors entering into real transactions every day.

The formal measurement system has not kept pace with this new global economy and the new ways in which value is created and realized. Let's look first at the problem by examining what makes up today's measurement system. It consists of the balance sheet (to recognize assets and liabilities), an income statement (to report revenues, expenses, gains, losses, and net income), and the cash flow statement (to report the sources and uses of cash flows). In Figure 2.1, the traditional financial reporting

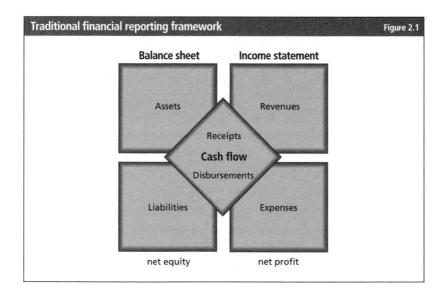

Traditional financial reporting framework   Figure 2.1

system is depicted with the balance sheet on the left, the income statement on the right, and the cash flow statement denoted in the middle.

Left out, of course, is most of the value created by intangible assets, including knowledge and relationships. This shortcoming affects the flow of information for decision-making by management and a company's stakeholders. Even worse, the balance sheet and income statement unwittingly pit human values against economic value. The income statement categorizes as "expenses" many of the most significant sources of value—people, for example—and overlooks much of the value derived from customer relationships and information (except for that arising from transactions during the period under review).

We have designed the Value Dynamics Framework (Figure 2.2) to identify and classify appropriately the assets of our time. The framework makes it possible for managers to better identify and leverage all of the assets essential to success in the New Economy—intangible as well as tangible. It supports managers in capturing more of the value within their organization, value that now lies untapped and unrecorded.

The Value Dynamics Framework includes traditional categories of physical and financial assets—so-called balance sheet assets. In addi-

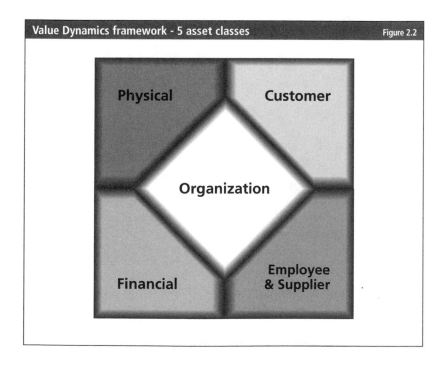

Value Dynamics framework - 5 asset classes   Figure 2.2

Physical

Customer

Organization

Financial

Employee
& Supplier

tion, we add three new groupings: Employee and supplier assets, customer assets, and organization assets. These new categories mainly comprise intangible assets, which have until now primarily been accounted for as expenses or providing revenues in the financial reporting system.

The Value Dynamics Framework also distinguishes between inbound and outbound relationship assets. Customers and market alliances are outbound from the company to the marketplace. The company's inbound relationships include employees and suppliers—the people and organizations that provide materials, products, and services.[2]

Companies create value by making the most of these tangible and intangible assets, different combinations of which form an organization's "economic DNA," if you will. By encompassing the full range of assets, Value Dynamics represents a major first step toward cracking the value code and seeing the organization as a whole. The Value Dynamics Framework thus provides a context for viewing the ways that organizations create value by combining and recombining different types of assets, tangible and intangible.

We can go a step further, however, by identifying the most significant assets within the five asset classes in Figure 2.3.

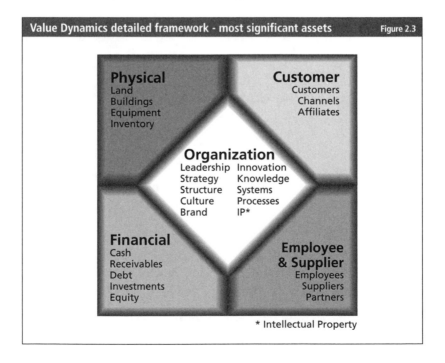

Value Dynamics detailed framework - most significant assets   Figure 2.3

Physical
Land
Buildings
Equipment
Inventory

Customer
Customers
Channels
Affiliates

Organization
Leadership   Innovation
Strategy   Knowledge
Structure   Systems
Culture   Processes
Brand   IP*

Financial
Cash
Receivables
Debt
Investments
Equity

Employee & Supplier
Employees
Suppliers
Partners

* Intellectual Property

We do not claim that this list of assets is all-inclusive. That's not its function. Your company makes investments in many different assets within these broad categories, depending on your unique requirements. Nevertheless, we believe that the 25 assets listed in the diagram are a good starting point for identifying and classifying the assets that matter to your organization's ability to create value.

Let's take a look at the ideas underlying the Value Dynamics Framework:

! Assets are both tangible and intangible.

The framework expands the definition of assets to include both tangible and intangible sources of value. By doing so, it encourages a new view of each asset's value proposition: People are no longer just expenses. Customers are more than sources of current or even future revenues. Balance-sheet assets—like factories and financial capital—are not the only assets that matter.

! Assets are defined more broadly as sources of future value.

We do not use the word asset in the manner prescribed by existing accounting rules. Instead, Value Dynamics defines assets as all potential sources of future economic benefit that have the capacity to contribute to a company's overall value. The definition thus expands the perspective on value creation.

! Assets are both owned and un-owned, controlled and not.

Conventional accounting definitions of assets are based on concepts of control and exclusivity. Value Dynamics holds that assets encompass sources of value both within a company's control and outside it. Sources of value, for example, may include not only a company's controlled assets, such its customer-focused Web site, but also customer and partner assets that the company neither owns nor controls.

! Assets in each category produce outputs.

The Value Dynamics Framework offers a guide for mapping the outputs produced by assets in all five asset classes. Physical assets for example, provide productive capacity, while financial assets provide various forms of capital and information. Customer assets provide information and money. Employee and supplier assets provide products and services, skills, and knowledge. Organization assets provide a range of outputs—from patented know-how to codified processes and systems.

! Assets have distinct life cycles.

Each asset has its own unique cost of acquisition, management, renewal, and disposition. Assets have economic lives with a beginning and an end. The framework provides a context for creating a risk and reward profile for each asset, as well as for the portfolio overall. It supports a focus on managing the life cycle of all assets.

! Assets must be managed to create, rather than destroy, value.

Assets have two faces. In a time of rapid change, they can quickly deteriorate, decreasing a company's market value. Alternatively, some assets may be extraordinary value-creators. Employees, for example, may use their skills to create value, but they may destroy a company's value if they are poorly motivated or have outdated skills. Similarly, a department store maintained long past its economic prime will be recorded on the balance sheet as an asset, when in reality it may be eroding the retailer's value.

! Assets include internal and external sources of value.

Companies use both internal and external assets in their business models. These include inbound assets such as supply chain partners and raw

> ## What is a company's economic DNA? All sources of value—tangible and intangible, internal and external to the enterprise.

materials, and all things outbound or in the marketplace, such as customers, channels, and brands. We redefine the asset base of a company to include many relationships external to the company itself.

! Value Dynamics creates a common language of value.

The framework supports the development of a common language for discussing both traditional and New Economy assets across corporate functions and skill sets. This helps people in various departments, as well as people in different disciplines, to exchange know-how that creates value.

To illustrate this framework in the world of business, let's start by looking at examples of companies leveraging different types of assets.

Q: Who is creating value with physical assets?
A: The Williams Companies, Inc.

Property has conferred the privileges of power and wealth for much of human history. Its tangible presence has assured owners of its reality. Physical assets—which includes property—are perhaps the most easily understood of our five asset categories. These assets include, as you might suspect, land, buildings, equipment, and inventory. Each holds the potential for adding value to a business. And this is especially true if you are creative.

Consider The Williams Companies, Inc.[3] Its senior managers came up with a novel way to make the most of one of its major physical assets—its miles and miles of pipeline. Williams, which employs some 21,000 people and is based in Tulsa, Oklahoma, is the largest-volume transporter of natural gas in the United States.

In 1984, with sales and profits plummeting, its senior managers sought new sources of income for the corporation. Among their initiatives was an all-out effort to identify alternate uses for its pipelines and their associated rights-of-way.

Keith E. Bailey, chairman, president, and chief executive officer, and his team came up with a winner: a plan to run fiber-optic lines through the pipelines and lease them to start-ups in the newly deregulated telecommunications industry.

The price advantage looked impressive: Pulling cable through an existing pipeline cut installation costs by about 40 percent—from $5 to $3 a foot.

The company began by snaking fiber-optic cables through some 660 miles of idle pipelines that linked Chicago, Illinois; Omaha, Nebraska; Kansas City, Kansas; and Des Moines, Iowa. That effort led to the birth of WinTel Network Services.

In 1994, Williams sold Wintel for $2.5 billion to what is now MCI WorldCom, Inc., headquartered in Clinton, Mississippi.

But Williams was unwilling to let go of an idea that had proven so profitable. After its three-year non-compete agreement with WorldCom

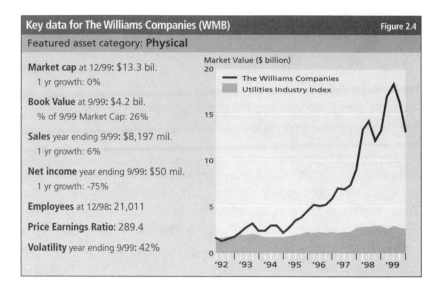

Key data for The Williams Companies (WMB)   Figure 2.4

Featured asset category: **Physical**

Market cap at 12/99: $13.3 bil.
  1 yr growth: 0%

Book Value at 9/99: $4.2 bil.
  % of 9/99 Market Cap: 26%

Sales year ending 9/99: $8,197 mil.
  1 yr growth: 6%

Net income year ending 9/99: $50 mil.
  1 yr growth: -75%

Employees at 12/98: 21,011

Price Earnings Ratio: 289.4

Volatility year ending 9/99: 42%

Market Value ($ billion)

— The Williams Companies
   Utilities Industry Index

expired, Williams reentered the wholesale communications business. The company is still very much in the natural-gas pipeline business, but it is, as Bailey puts it, "back—big time" in the business of selling wholesale capacity for carrying voice and data.

Williams now operates 19,490 route miles of installed fiber optic cable. And it has plans to extend the Williams Network to include a total of 33,120 route miles of fiber optic cable, using pipeline and other rights of way, to connect 125 cities by the end of the year 2000.

Williams, a natural gas transporter, is now "back—big time" in the business of selling fiber-optic capacity for voice and data.

Williams has already won contracts with U.S. West, Inc. (formerly U.S. West Communications Group and recently acquired by Qwest Communications International, Inc.), and Intermedia Communications, Inc.

Williams enjoyed a share price growth of 488 percent for the five years from mid-1994 through mid-1999. For the year ending the third quarter of 1999, Williams reported revenues of $8.2 billion and net income of $49.6 million. That's not bad for a company, which started out in gas pipelines and has moved into fiberoptics. (See Figure 2.4.)

Q: Who is creating value with financial assets?
A: The General Electric Company

At the dawn of history, people lived by barter, and it often took a series of trades back and forth to finally get a desired item. Later, currency made exchanges simpler and faster. The accepted currency of the day (shells, coins, or whatever) was used to "buy" an object directly.

Following that tradition, we define financial assets as currency, or things that give you rights to receive currency. These days virtually any asset can be converted to financial assets in the form of securities. Witness rock musician David Bowie's recent monetization of future royalties from his back catalog of songs.

In our model, financial assets include cash, receivables, investments, and sources of debt and equity. A financial asset is defined as such so long as it remains a source of capital and is capable of being exploited to create value.

The General Electric Company, based in Fairfield, Connecticut, has demonstrated a keen capacity for exploiting financial assets.[4]

When you think of General Electric, you probably think of physical objects, like light bulbs and refrigerators. Clearly, the assets that drive one of the world's most successful corporations are found mainly in its physical plant, right?

Not so.

The bottom line at General Electric shines bright largely because of the GE Capital Services subsidiary, which earns $55 billion in revenues annually —enough, if the subsidiary were independent, to give it 20th place on the Fortune 500 list.

In fact, the 28 businesses that make up GE Capital generate more than 40 percent of General Electric's net income. Without GE Capital, says Nicholas Heymann, an analyst at Prudential Securities, Inc., in New York, GE's sales would have risen only 4 percent annually from 1991 to 1996, instead of 9.1 percent.

As it was, GE's annual revenues through the end of the third quarter of 1999 exceeded $106.8 billion with net income approaching $10.3 billion.

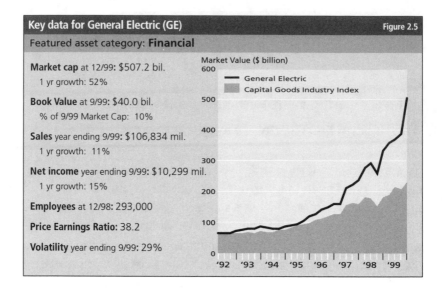

Key data for General Electric (GE)   Figure 2.5

Featured asset category: **Financial**

Market cap at 12/99: $507.2 bil.
  1 yr growth: 52%

Book Value at 9/99: $40.0 bil.
  % of 9/99 Market Cap: 10%

Sales year ending 9/99: $106,834 mil.
  1 yr growth: 11%

Net income year ending 9/99: $10,299 mil.
  1 yr growth: 15%

Employees at 12/98: 293,000

Price Earnings Ratio: 38.2

Volatility year ending 9/99: 29%

Market value tripled from year-end 1997 to December of 1999, and GE Capital was a big reason why that happened.

GE Capital began its prodigious rise in the 1930's as a subsidiary formed to help consumers finance the purchase of General Electric household appliances. A series of acquisitions, extensions, and start-ups made it into something else—a business juggernaut.

GE Capital is the largest equipment lessor on earth. Its assets include equipment leases that finance 750,000 cars, more than any car rental company; 188,000 rail cars, more than any railroad; 120,000 trucks, more than any overnight-delivery service; 900 aircraft, more than any commercial airline except Russia's Aeroflot; and 11 satellites, more than any television network.

The GE financial arm also handles commercial loans, residential mortgages, and copier financing for the Eastman Kodak Company, of Rochester, New York, and credit-card operations for Home Depot, Inc., in Atlanta, Georgia.

Of course, GE Capital benefits from the parent company's own strengths, among them top triple-A credit ratings, which give GE Capital an advantage in today's flush financial markets. But that would count for nothing if GE Capital's leaders hadn't known how to maximize the organization's financial assets to create new value for the company overall.

Q: Who is creating value with employee and supplier assets?
A: Starbucks Corporation

Employee and supplier assets take us beyond the balance sheet and its emphasis on things into the new world of Value Dynamics.

The most significant employee and supplier assets consist of employees, members of the supply chain, and partners. Each of the components in the employee and supplier asset category is considered a partner in producing products and services. All are part of the inbound chain of value creation. (This is in contrast to the outbound chain of assets, which includes customers and distributors.)

Starbucks Corporation has used its employee assets to achieve phenomenal market penetration almost overnight.[5] How fast is Starbucks growing? "I don't know for sure," quipped one comedian, "but I do know they just opened one in my living room."

Founded in Seattle, Washington, in 1971, the $1.7-billion-a-year chain—which takes its name from Starbuck, the coffee-loving first mate in Herman Melville's classic Moby Dick—is the world's number one specialty coffee retailer. It boasts over 2,100 outlets nationwide and opens a new store almost every day of the year. Fueling Starbucks' growth is a licensing agreement signed with Albertson's, Inc., to open coffee bars in more than 100 of its supermarkets across the United States in the year 2000.

"It's an ironic fact," says Howard Schultz, the company's chairman and chief executive officer, "that while retail and restaurant businesses live or die on customer service, their employees have among the lowest salaries and worst benefits of any industry. These people are not only the heart and soul but also the public face of the company. Every dollar earned passes through their hands."

Schultz asks: "If the fate of your business is in the hands of a 20-year-old, part-time worker who goes to college or pursues acting on the side, can you afford to treat him or her as expendable?"

The answer is obvious—at least to Schultz. He has made Starbucks

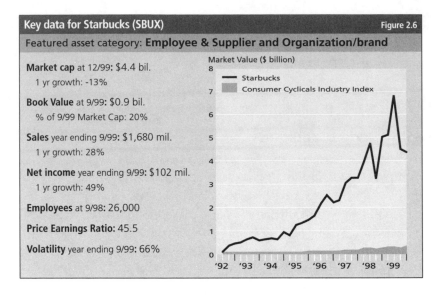

Key data for Starbucks (SBUX)   Figure 2.6

Featured asset category: **Employee & Supplier and Organization/brand**

Market cap at 12/99: $4.4 bil.
  1 yr growth: -13%

Book Value at 9/99: $0.9 bil.
  % of 9/99 Market Cap: 20%

Sales year ending 9/99: $1,680 mil.
  1 yr growth: 28%

Net income year ending 9/99: $102 mil.
  1 yr growth: 49%

Employees at 9/98: 26,000

Price Earnings Ratio: 45.5

Volatility year ending 9/99: 66%

Market Value ($ billion)
— Starbucks
▨ Consumer Cyclicals Industry Index

'92 '93 '94 '95 '96 '97 '98 '99

the restaurant and retail employer of choice by turning his company's generous benefits package into a key competitive advantage.

Starbucks pays more than the going wage in restaurants and retail stores and also offers benefits that are not provided elsewhere. Health insurance is available to everyone, including part-time employees.

So are stock options—or Bean Stock, as it is known. "The name," says Schultz, "isn't only a playful reference to the coffee beans we sell, but it also evokes Jack's beanstalk, which grew to the sky."

Viewed through the Value Dynamics lens, the stock options allow Starbucks to enhance employee assets as a source of value by giving people a direct interest in the company's total value.

The company's approach to maximizing its employee assets is paying off in an employee turnover rate that is far below that of comparable retailers (60 to 65 percent a year at Starbucks versus 150 to 400 percent elsewhere). Its store-manager-turnover rate (about 25 percent a year) is about half the industry average.

Q: Who is creating value with customer assets?
A: The Charles Schwab Corporation

Customers themselves are only one of the sources of value categorized in the Value Dynamics Framework as customer assets. What are the others? Distribution channels are one. Affiliates are another.

None are treated as assets by traditional accounting systems. And we believe this makes it difficult, if not impossible, to realize their potential as key weapons in a company's competitive arsenal.

To get a sense of what it means to maximize customer assets, consider, if you will, the corporate chameleon known as the Charles Schwab Corporation.

It was back in the dismal depths of the 1970s bear market that Charles Schwab first set up shop as a discount broker in San Francisco, giving customers a big break on their trades but refusing to tell them where to place their bets.[6] His business took off in the bull market of the next decade, mainly as a favorite of fairly sophisticated investors. His chief value-creating and intangible asset was a small, but growing customer base.

In the 1990s, Schwab found itself besieged by new customers who wanted help in placing their bets. The company responded to the challenge by offering customers all sorts of information about the market, and all sorts of programs to help them help themselves. By 1995, that loyal customer base had soared to 3.4 million active accounts, leaving its discount competitors in the dust.

That was the year Schwab once again broke ranks with its rivals to seize the advantage with e-commerce. Leveraging its customer assets by encouraging customers to trade on-line, Schwab drastically cut back its fixed costs. Today, more than half of all the company's trades are made on-line, and about 60 percent of new customers do business with schwab.com.

But the story isn't over. On December 4, 1998, the company found a new way to exploit its customer asset. To meet clients' demands for a

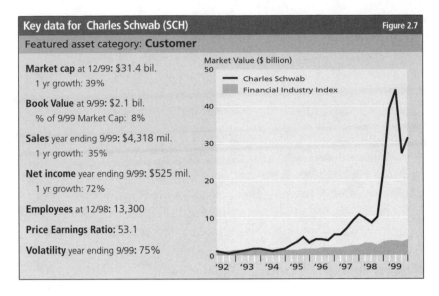

Key data for Charles Schwab (SCH) Figure 2.7

Featured asset category: **Customer**

Market cap at 12/99: $31.4 bil.
1 yr growth: 39%

Book Value at 9/99: $2.1 bil.
% of 9/99 Market Cap: 8%

Sales year ending 9/99: $4,318 mil.
1 yr growth: 35%

Net income year ending 9/99: $525 mil.
1 yr growth: 72%

Employees at 12/98: 13,300

Price Earnings Ratio: 53.1

Volatility year ending 9/99: 75%

Market Value ($ billion)
— Charles Schwab
Financial Industry Index

'92 '93 '94 '95 '96 '97 '98 '99

stake in the booming market for initial public offerings, Schwab for the first time became a co-manager for an IPO.

Schwab made for an attractive partner, given its huge, customer base of 6.4 million. Moreover, the company was able to use its on-line customer database to target its IPO Web sales efforts to clients most likely to be interested.

As of 1999, Schwab had parlayed its penchant for making the most of its customer assets into annual sales of more than $4.3 billion through the third quarter 1999, while net income reached $525 million. Even with a large correction during the last half of 1999, Schwab's market value was $31.4 billion at year-end.

To put it another way, if you had recognized Schwab's capacity for attracting and keeping customers and invested $1,000 in the company in 1987, your stake would have been worth $240,312 at century-end.

Q: Who is creating value with organization assets?
A: idealab!

Sometimes we overlook the trees because we are too enamored of the forest. Within the boundaries of a company's overall organizational system are a number of significant structural and intellectual assets not accounted for on the balance sheet.

In the Value Dynamics Framework, we call them organization assets, and we consider them to form the nervous system of a business. They allow one asset to work with another, one system to talk to another, and one decision to mesh with another.

Among key organization assets are leadership, strategy, structure, processes, systems, culture and values, ability to innovate, brands, and proprietary knowledge. They are largely intangible assets, though some can be codified or accorded legal protection with trademarks, patents, and the like.

Organization assets are key elements in building the relationships upon which the modern corporation relies—the association between managers and employees, between a company and its suppliers or its customers, even between its suppliers and customers themselves.

Managers who cannot identify, comprehend, and maximize these assets labor under a heavy handicap. But when they can exploit an organization asset like structure, the results can be startling and rewarding.

Witness the experience of idealab!, a Pasadena, California, company whose business is identifying, creating, and operating Internet businesses—again and again. At the simplest level, all corporations that franchise their businesses leverage organization assets, but idealab!'s approach is unusual.[7]

Launched in 1996, idealab! is dedicated to developing ideas into successful Internet-based businesses. As of 1999, more than 25 of these ideas had been loosed on the world.

What are these companies? They are ideas that evolve into stand-alone businesses within the environment that is idealab!. With a grubstake of up to $250,000 from idealab!, each operating company focuses on its core business proposition. idealab! provides on-going strategic counsel and resources, including office space and the accompanying network infrastructure, consulting and services relating to development and technology, graphic design, marketing, competitive research, legal, accounting and business development support.

What's different about idealab!'s entrepreneurial approach is that it surrenders the lion's share of the equity in each operating company to its management team and employees. Unlike parent companies that are loath to relinquish control of offspring and their revenue streams, idealab! thinks there's more to be gained by letting go.

That's because "the new math of ownership" is a terrific boost to human potential, says Bill Gross, founder and chief executive officer. Ownership incites higher performance, which in turn builds greater economic value which eventually translates to better returns for idealab!. idealab! is enabling one organization asset, structure, to enhance another, the capacity to innovate.

Salaries are modest, but every employee of an operating company receives an equity stake in the venture. The equity structure also limits the size of any operating company. Given the equity offering to employees, there can be no more than 100 workers, and there are usually far fewer.

That suits Bill Gross just fine. "Belonging to a small team exerts a basic emotional pull on employees," he says. It inspires loyalty, a cooperative spirit, and a dedication to common goals that boost performance enormously.

Gross acknowledges that his new math is counter-intuitive. "In a world where executive pay and prestige are still largely linked to the size of the [tangible] assets under one's control," he wrote in the *Harvard Business Review*, "the idea of relinquishing control represents a direct threat to a CEO."

In pursuit of his theory that worker-manager ownership and operational independence can work wonders, Gross has made the most of the organization assets at his disposal.

▶ What's next?

Companies of necessity combine and manage a broad range of assets in diverse ways to create (and destroy) value. The Value Dynamics Framework supports a new business model that optimizes that process, treating a company as a portfolio of assets, including technologies.

The next chapter looks at business models that have evolved in response to dramatic changes in the market.

Ask Yourself:

- List your company's most important assets in the five Value Dynamics asset classes: physical, financial, employee and supplier, customer, and organization.

- Does your organization recognize the value created from assets in these five categories?

- Is your company using new types of measurements to provide information about intangible assets? If so, which intangible assets?

- What would your company do if it discovered that the assets it thought were most enduring (physical assets, for example) would damage its future capability?

- Do the companies showcased in this chapter suggest to you new ways that your organization might enhance its physical, financial, employee and supplier, customer, and organization assets?

❑

3

Businesses Create Value with Different Business Models.

"The book of life is very rich . . . [it is all] written in the same language with the same code book. . . ."

— Carl Sagan[1]

George Orban was leading the good life back in 1996. Having succeeded as a retailer (among other things, he helped found a discount clothing chain called Ross Stores), Orban was taking a year-long sabbatical in Aix-en-Provence, an altogether charming town in the south of France.

But there was a fly in the ointment.

He was concerned about the performance of Egghead, a leading U.S. seller of hardware and software for personal computers, in which Orban had invested $500,000. Founded in Bellevue, Washington, and eventually headquartered in Spokane, Egghead had built its customer base by attracting sophisticated "early adopters" of new technologies.[2]

In 1992, Egghead had some 250 upscale boutiques, 2,500 employees, and annual revenues of $700 million. But since then, it had all been downhill. All sorts of companies—bookstores, office supply centers, superstores—were getting into personal computers, and peddling personal-computer peripherals as well as accessories and software at rock-bottom prices. On-line competitors were siphoning off still more business.

George Orban wasn't pleased, and as a board member of Egghead, he didn't hesitate to criticize management. In 1996, the other directors challenged the vacationing Orban to do better. In January 1997, he accepted the challenge and became chief executive officer.

By then Egghead was down to 77 stores and 1,000 employees, and it was losing money. Orban recognized the need for strong medicine, and he applied it. In 1998 he shut down all Egghead's stores, discharged four out of five employees, and put all Egghead's eggs into one basket, the Internet. As if to underline the finality of his decision, he renamed the company Egghead.com, Inc.

Largely freed of its bricks and mortar, Egghead.com increased its offerings to 100,000 products. Its Internet-based business expanded to three Web sites: One is for regular hardware and software products; another for liquidated goods; and a third for auctions of personal-computer wares. The company's much reduced overhead made it possible to compete with the world on price.

Orban's decision to entrust all of Egghead to the World Wide Web would probably be described as a "channel strategy" or "Internet play." Both characterizations would be accurate, but neither would tell the whole story.

Orban's genius was reflected in his willingness to act boldly when the value of Egghead's assets plummeted. From a Value Dynamics perspective, he slashed his investments in physical assets (storefronts) and redirected those resources to a different set of assets, including on-line relationships and knowledge. In the process, he radically transformed Egghead's business model.

This is not to imply that all eBusinesses can or should entirely abandon the physical world. As we will see in Part III, even virtual e-tailers like the Seattle-based bookseller, Amazon.com, are making significant investments in physical assets.

Although Egghead.com is still a work in progress, the initial results of Orban's actions are impressive. In its first year, the company's Web site realized revenues of more than $53 million. Egghead's market value had climbed to $500 million by January 2000, up from $150 million at the beginning of 1998.

In this chapter, we continue the journey toward value creation, asking yet again: How do organizations create value, anyway?

The answer: Companies create value, and incur risk, by assembling unique combinations of assets. It is this portfolio that we call the business model, and it determines a company's economic success.

Since the dawn of the Industrial Age, great entrepreneurs have found new ways, and used the latest technologies, to combine assets into business models of unique power. This is what distinguished entrepreneur-ial giants like the 18th-century English potter Josiah Wedgwood, automaker Henry Ford, and industrialist John D. Rockefeller.

For much of human history, economic growth was so gradual as to be almost imperceptible, and much of what growth was generated came in farming.[3] It was not until the mid-1700s that industrialization sparked an immense leap in productivity, which in turn led to astonishing increases in wealth and improvements in the quality of life.[4]

Figure 3.1 depicts historical periods linked to the prevailing tech-

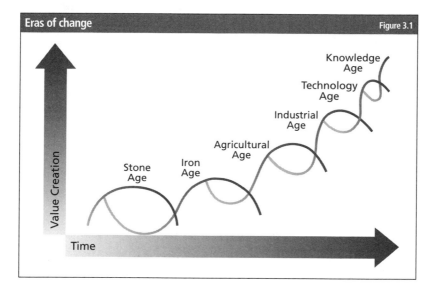

nologies of the time.[5] The pioneers of the British textile industry, for example, were merchants who figured out how to assemble radically new combinations of assets enhanced by a new technology of the Industrial Age, steam power.

These merchants invested in factories, machinery, and American cotton (that is, physical assets). They recruited a new urban workforce (employee assets), including women and children who hadn't worked for wages in the old agricultural economy. And they combined these assets in ways never before imagined, displaying an attention to detail and discipline (organization assets) previously seen only in the military.

In periods of economic transition, many organizations are carried along on the tide of new value creation, inventing new combinations and proportions of assets, which generate massive changes in the capacity to create value. Others resist the pull of the new models.

Andrew Carnegie, whose masterful use of new combinations of assets created enormous industrial value, described his father's refusal to convert to power-driven equipment, opting instead to continue weaving his damask on four hand-operated looms. "My father did not recognize the impending revolution and was struggling under the old system," Carnegie later wrote in his autobiography.[6]

Eventually, the newly automated weavers put William Carnegie out of business. But his son embraced breakthrough technologies like the telegraph, the railroad, and especially the Bessemer steelmaking process, amassing a fortune second only to that of Rockefeller.

The entrepreneurs of the New Economy—people like Microsoft's Bill Gates, Michael Dell, Charles Schwab, and Netscape's Jim Clark—are building fortunes using new combinations of assets. The rewards still go to those individuals and organizations that have the foresight and the ability to create business combinations never tried before. These new combinations also generate new risks, which can contribute to new levels of economic volatility.

Those companies that win the race to capture the new assets succeed in the marketplace, often assuming powerful "first mover" advantages. But they have another far-reaching effect—they eventually make commodities of old assets like physical goods, once scarce, but now abundant. Then, gradually, the new assets of one period become abundant and are themselves commoditized.

Companies are in a race to acquire the most valuable assets of our time.

Companies invest in tangible assets (like factories or warehouses) and intangible assets (like brands or systems) based on portfolio decisions to allocate resources in particular ways. In this sense, all business operating decisions are also investment decisions that affect value. Moreover, the resultant changes in a company's business model will influence its economic outcome, either positively or negatively.

In the pages that follow, we look at a host of companies in various industries that have invested in new sets of assets, and replaced yesterday's technologies with today's. By combining assets—their economic DNA—in entirely new ways, these companies are creating value.

Q: What company has reinvented its business model?
A: The Sara Lee Corporation.

Consider the Sara Lee Corporation, founded in 1939 and based in Chicago, Illinois. The company boasts 30 so-called mega-brands, meaning those with sales of more than $100 million annually.[7] They include Champion, Coach, Hanes, Hillshire Farm and Playtex. A division that makes its own food (like cheesecake) or clothing or other consumer good has long backed each of these brands.

In fact, Sara Lee, which posts sales of $20 billion and earnings of nearly $1 billion annually, was always vertically integrated. Its leaders proudly hailed that fact as an explanation for the company's success until September 15, 1997.

On that date, John H. Bryan, chief executive officer, announced that the corporation would stop manufacturing many of its products and become, in his words, an "asset-less company." Sara Lee, he said, would outsource its production to others and henceforth concentrate on extending the market reach of its brands.

We would not characterize Sara Lee as "asset-less." From our per-

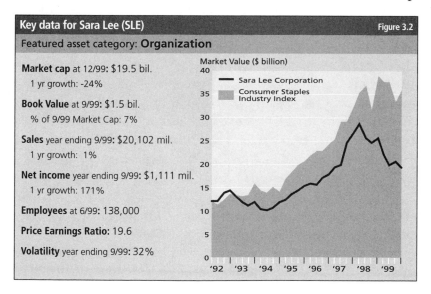

Key data for Sara Lee (SLE)   Figure 3.2

Featured asset category: **Organization**

Market cap at 12/99: $19.5 bil.
  1 yr growth: -24%

Book Value at 9/99: $1.5 bil.
  % of 9/99 Market Cap: 7%

Sales year ending 9/99: $20,102 mil.
  1 yr growth: 1%

Net income year ending 9/99: $1,111 mil.
  1 yr growth: 171%

Employees at 6/99: 138,000

Price Earnings Ratio: 19.6

Volatility year ending 9/99: 32%

Market Value ($ billion)

—— Sara Lee Corporation
▨ Consumer Staples Industry Index

spective, the company was redesigning its business model to decrease its emphasis on physical assets and increase its emphasis on brand assets.

The result? Sara Lee took a $1.6 billion restructuring charge in fiscal 1998, which led to a loss for the year. But the company also experienced an immediate (if temporary) $1.9 billion boost in its market capitalization, signaling strong support on Wall Street for the company's direction. The challenge for the company now is to take advantage of its most valuable assets and exploit the new structure to create success.

Q: What other companies have reinvented their business models?
A: The Coca-Cola Company and PepsiCo, Inc.

The year was 1981, and Roberto Goizueta had just become The Coca-Cola Company's chief executive officer. Coke and its chief rival, PepsiCo, Inc. each had approximately $4 billion in market capitalization. During the next two decades, both companies would redesign their asset portfolios more than once—with varying economic results.

Coca-Cola's business model in 1981 looked much as it had in the early part of the century. The company managed the brand centrally through national and regional advertising. It produced its "secret formula" syrup. Independent bottlers, which formed a franchise system, purchased the syrup at a fixed price, then blended syrups and concentrates with carbonated water for pouring into Coke's trademark cans, bottles, and fountains. The bottlers managed sales and distribution to the three key retail channels: grocery, fountain (restaurants), and vending machines.

Coca-Cola thrived. The company delivered Coke to more and more consumers every year, without large capital investment in the bottling operations. But by the 1970s, Coke's business model was showing signs of wear. Bottlers were now second and third generation—and had their eye on cash flow, more than growth. Markets had grown and become competitive. And Coke needed capital to expand into new markets, including international arenas.

In contrast, Pepsi-Cola Company was a division of PepsiCo, Inc., a diversified company that also owned the snack food giant Frito-Lay, Inc., a transportation company, and a sporting goods manufacturer. And because PepsiCo also owned many of its bottlers, Pepsi was better able to

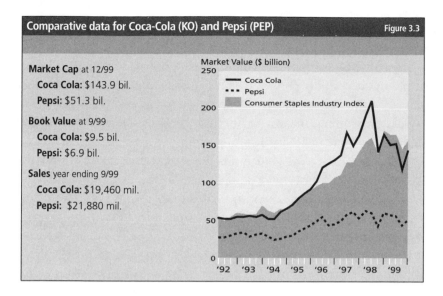

Comparative data for Coca-Cola (KO) and Pepsi (PEP)   Figure 3.3

Market Cap at 12/99
    Coca Cola: $143.9 bil.
    Pepsi: $51.3 bil.

Book Value at 9/99
    Coca Cola: $9.5 bil.
    Pepsi: $6.9 bil.

Sales year ending 9/99
    Coca Cola: $19,460 mil.
    Pepsi: $21,880 mil.

Market Value ($ billion)
—— Coca Cola
··· Pepsi
Consumer Staples Industry Index

capitalize on changes in distribution and retailing precipitated by the growth of regional and national supermarket chains in the United States.

To diversify into other growth businesses in the late 1970s, PepsiCo began to buy restaurant companies. It acquired two well-known, fast-food companies, Pizza Hut and Taco Bell. And in the mid-1980s, PepsiCo decided to focus on its three food businesses—beverages, snack foods, and restaurants. It sold the transportation and sporting goods business, and in 1986 purchased Kentucky Fried Chicken. From 1986 to 1996, as a result, PepsiCo's growth came not only from soft drinks, but also from food.

Coca-Cola, meanwhile, was adopting a new business model, one that called for an innovative strategy in relation to physical assets. Coca-Cola in 1986 consolidated the U.S. bottling operations, purchasing its two largest bottlers—JTL Corp. and BCI Holdings—to form Coca-Cola Enterprises (CCE). The new company went public immediately, with Coca-Cola keeping enough equity—49 percent—to maintain some control. The acquisition and subsequent IPO generated capital, which the company used for growth.

Goizueta engineered a success story during his tenure that would be hard to equal. During the 16 years under Goizueta's leadership, ending with his death in 1997, Coke's market capitalization grew more than 35-fold, from $4.3 billion to $153 billion in 1997, almost three times Pepsi's value.[8] While Coke was reaping financial rewards from leveraging its intangible assets (brand), PepsiCo had much of its asset portfolio weighted toward investments in fixed assets (restaurants and bottling plants).

The battle between these two giants isn't over, however. Just because a company successfully reinvents its business model once doesn't mean it won't be confronted regularly with the need for further change.

Coke was sailing in heavier seas as Doug Ivester, heir to Goizueta, resigned at the end of 1999 after only slightly more than two years as the company's CEO. Ivester's tenure was beset with problems with relationships with bottlers, customers, and other stakeholders—core intangible assets.[9] Coke's leadership came in for criticism from diverse sources, as the company fought antitrust actions in the United States and overseas. Coke's stock price fell behind the Standard & Poor's 500, and return on equity and profits dropped during the last two years of the century. Coke's market value was at $144 billion at year-end 1999. And early in the first year of the new millennium, Coca-Cola announced layoffs of 20 percent of its workforce and $1.6 billion in one-time charges.

As for PepsiCo, it is already reinventing its business model by spinning off its restaurants and focusing on core intangible assets, including brand and relationships. Its bottlers are now independent; they have formed the Pepsi Bottling Group.[10]

The lesson here is a simple one: No advantage, business model, or single asset lasts forever.

Q: What companies are using different business models in the computer industry?

A: Dell Computer and Compaq Computer Corporation.

How does it feel when the marketplace turns your name into a verb? Just ask Michael Dell of Dell Computer Corporation.

A group of business people and professors at Harvard University met some months back to talk about the Internet and the opportunities it presented. Not surprisingly, the conversation turned to the astonishing management shake-up at Compaq Computer Corporation, headquartered in Houston. Eckhard Pfeiffer, the company's once-renowned chairman and chief executive officer, was forced out in April 1999.

The consensus, according to a *Wall Street Journal* article, was that

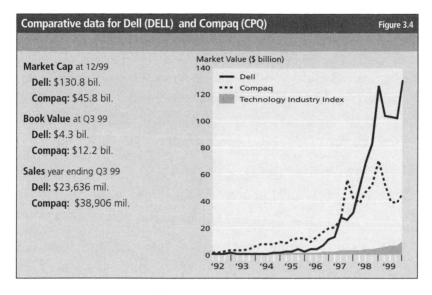

Comparative data for Dell (DELL) and Compaq (CPQ)   Figure 3.4

Market Cap at 12/99
Dell: $130.8 bil.
Compaq: $45.8 bil.

Book Value at Q3 99
Dell: $4.3 bil.
Compaq: $12.2 bil.

Sales year ending Q3 99
Dell: $23,636 mil.
Compaq: $38,906 mil.

Market Value ($ billion)

— Dell
▪▪▪ Compaq
Technology Industry Index

Pfeiffer had been "Delled."[11] In other words, Michael Dell and his eponymous company had managed to outmaneuver Compaq with edge-to-
edge digital power, brand strength, and keenly priced products—and this
despite Compaq's significant investment in physical and financial assets.

How did Dell do it?

The company—as we explained in Chapter 1—used direct-to-cus-
tomer phone sales and service to best its competition. It eliminated
middlemen dealers and expensive inventories, and passed the savings
along to customers. That's particularly important in an industry in
which core product prices are dropping an average of 30 percent a year.

Then, when competitors imitated its winning ways, Dell reinvented
itself, beginning to rely on a system of suppliers linked by long-term
contracts and information networks.

Looking at the company's success from a Value Dynamics perspective, Dell created a business model with significant investment in supplier assets, which it then linked to its customer assets, using the Internet
and its organizational know-how and systems.

In fact, Dell's reengineering to enable customers to access sales and
service on its Web site has allowed the company to become even more
successful. Its direct business model eliminates the distribution network
that had separated Dell from its customers. Its network of linked suppliers makes it possible for the company to efficiently tailor its computer
products to fit the needs of individual buyers.

Dell's competitors aren't giving up, of course. Compaq is fighting hard to keep pace, not least by buying companies like Digital Equipment Corporation. And the departure of Pfeiffer in mid-1999 points to Compaq's determination to regroup around revitalized organization assets—a new strategy and leadership team.

Q: What companies use business models with differing
**   degrees of scalability?**

A: Simon Property Group, Inc. and America Online, Inc.

Simon Property Group, Inc., based in Indianapolis, Indiana, is the largest real estate company in North America. The company itself isn't a household word, but shoppers make a staggering 2.3 billion visits to its malls every year, including the famed Mall of America in Minneapolis, Minnesota. Now it is moving into cyberspace as a way to tap into a hugely expanded universe of customers—to improve its scalability when it comes to assets.[12]

It all started in 1955 when Mel and Herb Simon had an idea that would change shopping forever—bring shoppers and retailers under a single roof and call it a mall. As the geniuses behind modern mall shopping, the Simon brothers, in effect, created a physical portal where customers could browse, chat, and shop. That idea spawned a shopping empire that now encompasses 259 regional malls, community shopping centers, and mixed-use properties. The company manages 184 million square feet of space.

Simon Property is organized as a real estate investment trust (REIT), and has, until recently, defined its business model primarily in terms of physical assets—square feet under management and retail space rented. Not directly counted as assets in its business model are the consumers who pass through its doors to visit the mall's retailers, nor the almost three-quarters of a million retailing employees who work in these malls.

Compare the Simon business model with that of America Online (before its announced merger with Time Warner). AOL serves its customers in many ways, but it might be considered something of an online version of a shopping mall, an electronic portal through which unlimited numbers of consumers can browse, chat, and shop.

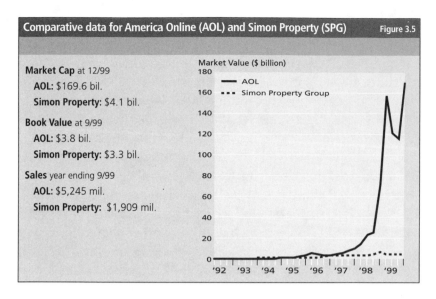

Comparative data for America Online (AOL) and Simon Property (SPG)   Figure 3.5

Market Cap at 12/99
  AOL: $169.6 bil.
  Simon Property: $4.1 bil.

Book Value at 9/99
  AOL: $3.8 bil.
  Simon Property: $3.3 bil.

Sales year ending 9/99
  AOL: $5,245 mil.
  Simon Property: $1,909 mil.

Market Value ($ billion)
— AOL
∙∙∙ Simon Property Group

AOL, which employs 12,100 people, is squeezing big dollars out of retailers, advertisers, publishers, programmers, and anyone else trying to reach the millions of eyeballs that scan AOL every day.

For example, Cendant Corporation, in Parsippany, New Jersey, paid $50 million for AOL to carry its on-line discount-shopping service. Preview Travel, Inc., of San Francisco, paid $32 million to become the service's on-line travel agent. Meanwhile, N2K, Inc., based in New York City, paid $18 million—twice its annual revenues—to become the sole music retailer, and Intuit, Inc., (the originator of Quicken) based in Mountain View, forked over $30 million to sell financial services.

The lure of AOL's customer base is such that Internet powerhouse Amazon.com, paid $19 million to become the bookseller on AOL's Web site, while its competitor, New York's Barnes & Noble, Inc., paid $40 million to be the exclusive book retailer inside AOL.

AOL has fewer customers than Simon Property, fewer locations (primarily its Dulles, Virginia, headquarters), and less capital invested. But a mall's access to customers is traditionally rooted in physical locations, which makes it less easily scalable than the customer assets and electronic offerings gathered under AOL's spreading wings. (AOL's proposed merger with Time Warner would take those offerings even further, creating a conduit between on-line subscribers and vast media properties.)

Though the two companies have similar book values, AOL's market value is more than 40 times that of Simon Property. (See Figure 3.5.)

Simon Property had a market capitalization of approximately $4.1 billion as of year-end 1999,[13] whereas AOL, the first Internet company to join the S&P 500, had a market value of $169.6 billion.

What distinguishes these two business models is "scalability"—one of the most important drivers of value in the New Economy.

What is scalability? Consider a software firm. The company invests large amounts of money into research and development to create a single software application, codifying large amounts of knowledge into a product delivered in a variety of formats, including downloading from the Internet. The product itself can be replicated for pennies. Thus the product can be scaled for offering across diverse channels of distribution to large numbers of customers. Or a single Internet platform can serve a large community of users, offering everything from e-mail to e-commerce. The site is usable by one person or millions. In other words, technology enables assets and business models to be scaled to encompass more than just a single product, physical location, or customer.

Let's revisit Simon because the story is far from over for this mall owner. The company has begun adjusting its business model, taking stock of its supplier and customer assets, and considering how to create stronger linkages among them, using new strategies and technologies to create value.

Late in 1997, the company formed a wholly owned subsidiary, Simon Brand Ventures, whose key mission is to use Simon's vast customer base to implement mall marketing initiatives. The business has concluded marketing and technology alliances with the likes of VISA International, Americash Mall, Inc., Smartalk Teleservices, and Diebold, Inc., among others, to promote goods and services directly to retailers and consumers. Simon Brand Ventures is moving to enhance the value of the company's customer assets.

At the same time, David Simon, the family's next generation, has become one of the authors of a new business model dubbed "clicks and bricks." In other words, the company has begun moving into cyberspace. It has tapped Melanie Alshab, formerly a senior vice president and chief information officer, to head Clixnmortar.com ("Clix"), a new Simon subsidiary. A pair of new Web services—Fastfrog.com and Yoursherpa.com—are among the first offerings.

Fastfrog.com allows teens to go to a Simon-owned mall, check in at a kiosk called "The Pad," and borrow a scanner about the size of a small TV remote to carry from shop to shop. These young shoppers can then scan product bar codes of desired products into the device's memory. When they return to the pad, information about the scanned products goes right into the Clix system for e-mailing to parents and friends. The e-mail recipients choose to buy the item and have it shipped, make the purchase at the mall, or simply say "no." Yoursherpa.com is a more sophisticated version of Fastfrog.com for adults.

Simon has also formed a division to sell high-speed Internet and telecommunications services to its retail tenants. Simon is partnering with Intermedia Communications Inc., Tampa, Florida; Copper Mountain Networks Inc., Palo Alto, California; and a third, yet-to-be-named telecom company, to wire up its malls to provide Internet and "extranet" services to its retailers.

Clearly, the more broadly Simon adapts its business model to the Internet, the more closely its scalability will approach that of AOL. The goal for both—to use the widest possible array of technologies to create the most successful business models in retailing.

Now it's your turn. Let's say you have been given $1 million to build your company's business model. You know that assets are the core building blocks of value, and that wise investment in the various assets is critical.

You also know that certain technologies can make assets scalable—using the Internet to expand the value-producing capabilities of real estate, for example. Networking and connectivity, too, can increase an asset's power to create value. So can relationships that facilitate an open two-way exchange of information.

Given these facts, how would you spend your funds? Would you use the capital to acquire new locations or gain access to more customers? Should some of those financial assets go into new processes and systems? How about putting them into training your employees and developing their competencies? Might you invest it in plant, property, and equipment? Or would you put the money in the bank as part of your cash reserves? You only have $1 million, so your decisions are important. Time and resources are finite.

Now think about how your company currently makes these decisions. Is it on a trajectory of success? Or does the way it invests in a portfolio of tangible and intangible assets make course corrections essential?

As David Bohnett, founder of GeoCities, an Internet company acquired by Yahoo!, has said: "We are paranoid because we don't want anyone doing to us what we did to others"—that is, make their business model obsolete.[14] Remember, successful business models are fleeting, because asset values do not last forever.

▶ What's next?

In the first three chapters we have looked at assets and business models, and shown how companies can thrive or languish based on their allocation of resources among tangible and intangible assets. Our conclusion is that companies need to *see* what matters (all of their assets) and *invest in* what matters (the optimal combination of assets).

To that end, we offer Value Dynamics, a new set of principles for value creation, and a way for companies to classify all of their important assets into five broad categories.

The next five chapters showcase companies that excel at using a particular asset as a building block of value. We examine through individual case studies the assets we have identified as being most significant in the Value Dynamics Framework.

Please note, we are not suggesting that our showcased companies are using only one asset to create value. Quite the contrary. We highlight a specific asset merely to spur your thinking about your organization's assets and new ways to invest in them to create value.

We cannot yet correlate the economic contributions of these assets with market value because of the deficiencies of our current measurement systems. Still, the highlighted companies do provide valuable examples. Identifying the assets that matter is the first step toward cracking the value code.

We begin in the next chapter with the assets that usually come to mind when assets are mentioned—that is, physical assets. We define the most important components in the physical asset grouping and show you how industry giants are exploiting these assets in ways that make competitors tremble.

Ask Yourself:

- Does your company excel at using one type of asset as opposed to others? What assets does your company use to enhance the value of the rest of your portfolio?

- Is your company's business model changing? Are the changes being initiated in response to traditional competitors or to the market at large?

- What impact have other organizations' changing business models had on your company's market value? What is that impact likely to be over the next few years?

- How is the Internet changing your company's business model? What new competitors are even now seeking to destroy your business?

Invest in What Matters

4

Who is Creating Value with Physical Assets?

"Sooner or later, you need more than an outpost in cyberspace. When you have a problem affecting customers, that's when you know the true meaning of the word 'mortar.' "

— David S. Pottruck[1]

J ust how big is Wal-Mart Stores, Inc.?

Think about the giant retailer, the world's largest, this way: Each year, Wal-Mart pockets $1 out of every $5 spent in U.S. retail stores.[2]

It also sells enough socks and underwear annually to put a new pair on every man and woman in the country—with some to spare.

Wal-Mart didn't reach this pinnacle of business success by resting on its assets. The people who run this ever-expanding chain of more than 3,600 stores always search for new ways to do what they have long done best—that is, cut costs and use their assets to their greatest advantage.

A case in point is Wal-Mart's use of its physical assets—specifically, the restaurants that operate within its walls.

In-store restaurants are nothing new, of course. Retailers have fed hungry customers for generations, starting, at least in the United States, with lunch counters at the F. W. Woolworth Company's five-and-ten-cent stores. The theory was that if people ate where they shopped, they would see more products and buy more of what they saw, boosting overall sales. Moreover, the in-store restaurants might themselves post a profit.

From the start, Wal-Mart—which had annual sales to the third quarter of 1999 of more than $154.4 billion and net income of $5.2 billion—installed snack bars in most of its stores. These snack bars accounted for some $47 million of the company's profits in 1992.

That was the year McDonald's Corporation sent a team of managers from its Oak Brook, Illinois, headquarters to Wal-Mart's home office in Bentonville, Arkansas. Their aim was to see what operations lessons Wal-Mart executives could teach the world's leading fast-food service provider, with more than 24,000 restaurants worldwide.

Physical assets are accounted for on the balance sheet. But book value isn't a good guide to market value.

McDonald's managers got more than they expected. One conversation led to another. McDonald's managers told their Wal-Mart counterparts about the kind of sales their restaurants were generating in other retail stores.

It didn't take Wal-Mart executives long to see that they could win by renting out their snack-bar space to the Big Mac brigade. For one, Wal-Mart could obtain a steady flow of cash and eliminate the cost of its snack-bar operations. Then the higher McDonald's sales climbed, the higher the rent Wal-Mart could collect and the higher Wal-Mart's revenues per square foot. What is more, the plan would allow Wal-Mart to enhance the experience of its customers, long one of its primary objectives. A McDonald's was bound to keep customers in the store longer than a snack bar ever could—and it might even lure new ones. Also, a joint venture between the two companies offered opportunities for cooperative sales promotions.

So, in January 1993, McDonald's opened its first restaurant in a Wal-Mart. Today, more than 800 Wal-Mart stores boast a McDonald's.

The substitution of McDonald's restaurants for Wal-Mart snack bars is an example of the subject of this chapter—how to make the most of an organization's physical assets (in this case, Wal-Mart's buildings). How the giant retailer treats another physical asset—its inventory—illustrates the topic of the chapter as well.

Inventory is anathema to Wal-Mart. Some 80 percent of the retailer's costs come from in-store operations, and inventory represents a large portion of those expenses. The chain wants to reduce, if not eliminate, its inventory, and it has found a way to begin accomplishing that goal. Wal-

Mart is persuading its suppliers to deliver their goods in a form that permits store employees to wheel them directly from truck to shelf or selling floor. That way, products don't sit in the back room out of the view of customers.

Ready-made store displays—dubbed PDFs, short for "pretty darn fast" displays—are what Wal-Mart wants from its suppliers. It also wants products like grills and bikes pre-assembled, and clothing delivered on hangers with price tags attached.

An ideal supplier display—at least in the eyes of Wal-Mart managers—has the product's brand name emblazoned upon it to get attention. Many of the PDF displays also include everything a customer might want to know about a product, such as how much it costs, how to use it, and how to clean it. That means there is no need for a Wal-Mart employee to explain things.

All that, Wal-Mart managers believe, leads to savings on inventory, which makes it possible to slash prices even more. The PDF displays also free workers from tasks they often dislike—such as assembling products and tracking inventory. Wal-Mart has realized that the ultimate way to make the most of its inventory, a physical asset, is to do away with it.

Now, we aren't suggesting that Wal-Mart makes the most of its physical assets and only its physical assets. Even our two examples

eBusiness is about integrating the old and the new—what we call "clicks and bricks."

show the company benefiting from its supplier assets as well as its physical ones.

But our topic here is physical assets. So, in the pages that follow, we show how a variety of companies—among them, Dell Computer Corporation, The Walt Disney Company, and Southwest Airlines Company—are making the most of physical assets.

Let's clarify what we mean by physical assets.

The category includes land, buildings, equipment, and inventory—in other words, things you can see and touch. You can count them, even weigh them. Physical assets are central to strategic decisions about the security of a company's raw-materials supply, its real estate investments, its productive capacity, even its finished goods inventory.

Physical assets are what most of us think of when we hear the term tangible assets. And every company in every industry has them—even predominantly virtual ones, like financial-services innovator Charles Schwab.

Listen to David S. Pottruck, co-chief executive officer of Schwab. The future of eBusiness, he often argues, won't be about the physical versus the virtual, but about integrating the best of both in what is known around Schwab as "clicks and mortar™." [3]

"It's a false dichotomy to think you're either doing business on-line or you're doing it in the old-fashioned way. We're all embedded in the real world," he noted at a recent Internet conference.

Schwab rings up some $10 billion a week in e-commerce transactions. It also operates 337 branch offices and four national service centers. And it has announced plans to expand its network of branch offices—that is, its physical assets.

Physical assets are measured and accounted for on the balance sheet. Book value, though, is often not a good guide to the market value of these assets. And it doesn't show whether they create value for a business or detract from its overall worth. Land and buildings, for instance, frequently sell for much more than the amount carried on a company's books. Likewise, the market value of a four-year-old computer system is usually lower than its book value.

Let's look at these physical assets one by one. Remember, none of the companies detailed here maximizes physical assets alone.

🅠 How do we define land?

Land has always had a certain mystique. Countries go to war over it. Neighbors build fences to keep one another from setting foot on it. Farmers and ranchers pride themselves on being close to it. We define land as a piece of real estate held for productive use or investment. We also include land improvements. Why? Raw land without roads, utility connections, and the like is worthless in most business situations.

Q: Who is creating value with land?

A: The Walt Disney Company.

In 1954, when Walt Disney, the storied founder, chairman, and chief executive officer of The Walt Disney Company, based in Burbank, California, bought 160 acres in Anaheim, California, for his proposed Disneyland, he was short of cash.[4] He had hoped to buy more land, but he was already burdened with substantial debt. Also, he was concerned about construction costs.

Disney later said he regretted not purchasing additional acreage. And his regret grew after his park became surrounded by fast-food restaurants and motels. So when the decision was made to go forward with the construction of Disney World in Orlando, Florida, Disney opted for a different course. Free of cash considerations, his company purchased 29,500 acres. The average price was $200 an acre.

Today, less than half that land is in use. The rest has increased in value to a $1 million an acre or more. In fact, if Disney chose to sell its undeveloped land, it would pocket $15 billion. That is a hefty sum, even for Disney, which boasted annual sales through the third quarter of 1999 of some $23.4 billion, net income of $1.3 billion, and a market value of $60.4 billion at year-end 1999. (See Figure 4.1.)

But the land is worth more to Disney than even its market value indicates. That is because it is vital to the success of Disney's theme parks.

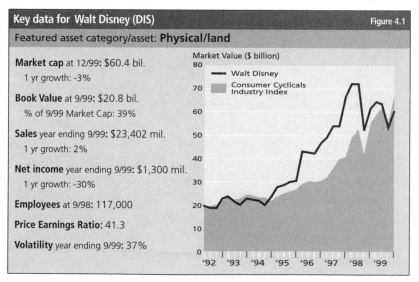

Key data for Walt Disney (DIS)   Figure 4.1

Featured asset category/asset: **Physical/land**

Market cap at 12/99: $60.4 bil.
1 yr growth: -3%

Book Value at 9/99: $20.8 bil.
% of 9/99 Market Cap: 39%

Sales year ending 9/99: $23,402 mil.
1 yr growth: 2%

Net income year ending 9/99: $1,300 mil.
1 yr growth: -30%

Employees at 9/98: 117,000

Price Earnings Ratio: 41.3

Volatility year ending 9/99: 37%

Market Value ($ billion)

— Walt Disney
Consumer Cyclicals Industry Index

'92 '93 '94 '95 '96 '97 '98 '99

Ⓠ How do we define a building?

Webster's defines a building as any structure with a roof or walls that is built for permanent use. However, we define a building, consistent

> ## Wal-Mart, the giant retailer, demonstrates how physical assets—buildings and inventory specifically—can add dramatically to value.

with accounting conventions—any tangible structure that most often is permanently attached to the land on which it sits and is usable for human habitation.

So we include factories, offices, and warehouses in our definition. We don't, however, distinguish between design or type of materials used. Why? Just about any building can be used to create value if it is properly managed.

Remember, our research suggests that buildings and other physical assets are declining in value relative to intangible assets. So managers need to determine carefully how these assets can create value and in what ways. Wal-mart is one company that excels at just that.

Ⓠ How do we define equipment?

Every carpenter knows the value of having the right equipment. So does almost every business person. But as any carpenter can tell you, tools are worthless if you don't know how to use them. The companies we feature here not only know how to use their equipment, they also know how to enhance its use in ways that create value.

We define equipment as a machine or tool employed to complete a particular task. It can be anything from a popcorn popper to a printing press. It includes computer hardware and other digital-age equipment. But we don't classify the codified knowledge embedded in computer software and systems as equipment. It is an organization asset.

Q: Who is creating value with equipment?
A: Southwest Airlines Company.

In some respects, Southwest Airlines Company, based in Dallas, Texas, running some 2,500 flights daily to 55 cities in 29 states, is like any other airline: Its fleet of more than 300 aircraft is its primary physical asset.[5]

But Southwest differs from its rivals in a key way: It operates just one kind of plane, the fuel- and cost-efficient Boeing 737, manufactured by the Boeing Company of Seattle, Washington.

By limiting its equipment to 737s, Southwest has simplified operations and, consequently, reduced costs. Its approach to its physical assets also enables it to make the most of its employee and supplier assets—that is, its pilots, ground crews, and other employees. Let us count the ways.

One, only a single parts inventory is needed.

Two, ground crews get to know the Boeing 737 inside and out, which translates into speedier, more efficient flight servicing.

Planes spend less time at airport stopovers (an average of 15 to 20 minutes versus nearly an hour at other carriers) and more time in the sky (an average of 11 hours and 7 minutes a day versus 7 hours and 14 minutes a day at other airlines).

Three, training of employees—from pilots and flight crews to mechanics—is faster since they don't need to learn about a variety of air-

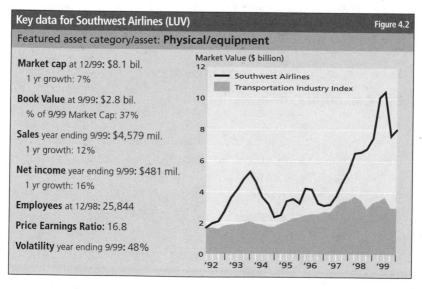

Key data for Southwest Airlines (LUV) — Figure 4.2

Featured asset category/asset: **Physical/equipment**

Market cap at 12/99: $8.1 bil.
  1 yr growth: 7%

Book Value at 9/99: $2.8 bil.
  % of 9/99 Market Cap: 37%

Sales year ending 9/99: $4,579 mil.
  1 yr growth: 12%

Net income year ending 9/99: $481 mil.
  1 yr growth: 16%

Employees at 12/98: 25,844

Price Earnings Ratio: 16.8

Volatility year ending 9/99: 48%

Market Value ($ billion)
— Southwest Airlines
  Transportation Industry Index
'92 '93 '94 '95 '96 '97 '98 '99

craft. Any airplane and flight crew can easily be substituted for another.

Making the most of its equipment is paying off at Southwest. Other airlines spend about 9.5 cents per seat mile and report a profit margin of about 4 percent. Southwest lays out about 7.5 cents per seat mile, and its profit margin exceeds 6 percent.

The company, which is the fourth largest U.S. domestic airline, had revenues for the year ending the third quarter of 1999 of more than $4.6 billion and net income of some $481 million in the same period. It is now the most consistently profitable and rapidly growing airline in the United States. (See Figure 4.2.)

That fact isn't lost on investors. They had driven up Southwest's market capitalization to $8.1 billion as of January 1, 2000. Even with a market value decline occurring in third quarter of 1999, Southwest outperformed its industry significantly. The company's price-to-earnings ratio, as of the third quarter of 1999, stood at 16.8 to 1.

🅠 How do we define inventory?

We define inventory as items of tangible property that are held for sale in the ordinary course of business, are used in the process of production, or are to be consumed to produce products or services. Inventory includes finished goods, partly finished goods, or work in process. It also includes raw materials that become part of a company's product, and supplies used in the normal course of a company's operations.

Q: Who is creating value with inventory?
A: Dell Computer Corporation.

Given the unpredictability and sudden changes that plague its industry, Dell Computer Corporation has to be ready to move on a moment's notice. It needs to be ready to move its inventory.

Inventory or, more specifically, lack of inventory determines profits. Inventory management is integral to the company's strategy of owning as little as possible.

Dell, like Wal-Mart, has realized that the ultimate way to make the most of its inventory is to eliminate as much of it as possible.

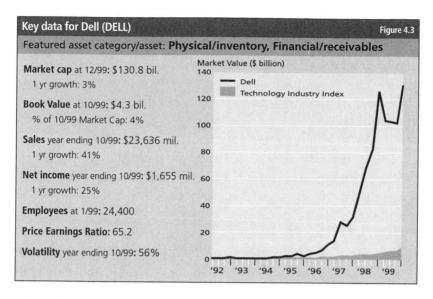

Key data for Dell (DELL)   Figure 4.3

Featured asset category/asset: **Physical/inventory, Financial/receivables**

Market cap at 12/99: $130.8 bil.
  1 yr growth: 3%

Book Value at 10/99: $4.3 bil.
  % of 10/99 Market Cap: 4%

Sales year ending 10/99: $23,636 mil.
  1 yr growth: 41%

Net income year ending 10/99: $1,655 mil.
  1 yr growth: 25%

Employees at 1/99: 24,400

Price Earnings Ratio: 65.2

Volatility year ending 10/99: 56%

Market Value ($ billion)

— Dell
▓ Technology Industry Index

Here, less is definitely more.

How does Dell do it?

This direct marketer of personal computers keeps close track of inventory velocity—that is, how fast various parts provided by suppliers can be turned into Dell computers and moved out the door to paying customers. In this way, Dell capitalizes on both its inventory and its suppliers.

At Dell, every computer component carries a printed four-digit code: For example, a processor board labeled "99-34" was created in the thirty-fourth week of 1999. At the point of assembly, the processor board is checked to determine the time it took to go from supplier to finished personal computer.

The elapsed time is the inventory velocity. Why is this figure so important? The greater the velocity, the smaller the inventory.

"Think about it this way," Michael S. Dell, the company's founder, chairman, and chief executive officer, told the *Harvard Business Review*,

Dell realized that the best way to manage inventory was to eliminate as much as possible.

"Assets collect risks. Inventory carries risk. If the cost of materials goes down 50 percent in a year, and you have two or three months of inventory versus 11 days, you've got a big cost disadvantage." He added, "In our business, if you don't move fast, you're out of the game."

Dell Computer's managers pay attention—on a weekly basis—to inventory velocity and the number of days of total inventory. Both figures are calculated by product and component, and distributed to Dell's entire management team.

In 1997 Dell inventory velocity stood at 7 days, with a total inventory at 13 days, compared to 75 to 100 days for competitors who sell their computers through retail stores. In 1998 inventory velocity was down to 3 days, with total inventory at 7 days, versus 80 or more days for Dell's competitors.

While Dell's inventory velocity has been speeding up, its earnings have been soaring. And its investors have taken note: The company's stock price grew 72,400 percent during the decade of the 1990s. Dell's performance was particularly strong in the two years ending December 31, 1999, quadrupling in value. (See Figure 4.3.)

▶ What's next?

In the next chapter, which deals with financial assets, we encounter other companies that are creating value in the New Economy. But this time we examine how businesses are making the most of their cash and other financial assets that can readily be converted into cash. Cash, after all, is crucial to every business in every industry.

Ask Yourself:

- Is your company effectively managing its physical assets to create value? Consider each of the primary physical assets—land, buildings, equipment and inventory.

- Think of the companies you know. Do any of these organizations excel at using physical assets to create value? How does your company stack up against these organizations? How does it stack up against its competitors?

- Do the case studies of companies presented in this chapter suggest ways that your company might manage physical assets more effectively?

- Can you conceive of any new strategies to make the most of your company's physical assets?

- What are your industry's best practices for managing physical assets?

5

Who is Creating Value with Financial Assets?

"The first $20 million is always the hardest."

— Po Bronson[1]

In 1994, Robert B. Shapiro, chairman and chief executive officer of the Monsanto Company, a life-sciences giant based in St. Louis, Missouri, gathered together some of his best and brightest people. He pulled them from every part of his organization. Telling them to think big, he asked them to consider the world today, the major trends, then suggest a role Monsanto might play in that future.

Shapiro's charge didn't go unheard. His call inspired a dramatic new (some would say even controversial) mission for the company—to help combat what he and his colleagues saw (and see) as a global environmental crisis brought on by unsustainable production practices and the world's burgeoning population.

Subsequently Monsanto was restructured to promote a vision of "sustainable development" for the world. Since then the company has sold off what was the heart of its operations, its $3-billion chemicals division. At the same time, it has hired molecular biologists by the score and sponsored far-ranging research into the DNA of plants. It has also spent billions to buy businesses that are on the forefront of biotechnology.

How could Monsanto afford all this?

It is reinvesting a financial asset—specifically, the cash flow produced in large part by a single product, its herbicide Roundup. By itself, Roundup accounted for 40 percent of Monsanto's operating profits. In

1998 those profits (meaning after-tax income from continuing operations, excluding unusual items) amounted to $580 million. Revenues
stood at $8.6 billion.

The future for Monsanto in particular and business in general,
Shapiro argues, isn't about making more material things—"stuff," as he
calls it—that the earth's environment cannot sustain. Rather, it is about
creating "smart" products—miniaturized or otherwise reconfigured

In our model, financial assets include cash, receivables, investments, and relationships with providers of debt and equity.

products that will help alleviate the waste that he and his colleagues
believe is choking the world. These products, he maintains, will be built
on proprietary technology.

Investors approve. They have responded to the company's actions
by bidding up the price of its common stock to the point where Monsanto's market capitalization of $22.5 billion, at year-end 1999, is more
than four times its book value.[2]

Put another way, Monsanto is using its financial assets to create
value for all its stakeholders. With eyes fixed on the road ahead, the
company's managers are riding their biotechnology investment right
into the future.

In this chapter, we explore how Microsoft, Cisco Systems, Inc., and
Lucent Technologies Inc., among others, are also making the most of
their financial assets.

First, though, a few definitions.

We include in financial assets cash and cash flow, receivables, investments, and relationships with providers of debt and equity. These assets
aren't the only ones in the financial category. But they have significant
influence on an organization's financial status, its credit and investment
worthiness, and its general ability to attract funds.

🅠 How do we define cash?

We define cash as currency on hand. We also include demand deposits with banks or other financial institutions, as well as other kinds of accounts that have the same characteristics as demand deposits.

Responsible money management today requires that any temporary excess amount of cash be put to use earning more money, even if only for a day or two. So companies invest idle cash in highly liquid short-term investments like money market funds and U.S. Treasury bills. These are known as cash equivalents.

How do we define cash flow? Companies such as PepsiCo, Inc., for example, focus on cash flow or more particularly free cash flow, which is the amount left over after providing working capital to the company's businesses, making investments, and paying dividends and interest. Under the leadership of Roger A. Enrico, PepsiCo's chairman and chief executive officer, free cash flow from the company's operations nearly doubled in 1997 to some $1.4 billion. In his 1998 Chairman's Letter, he said operating cash flow from the company's core packaged goods business surpassed $2 billion, which was being using to reduce debt, repurchase stock, and invest in new business opportunities.[3]

Q: Who else is creating value with cash?

A: Microsoft Corporation.

When Bill Gates stepped down from his post as chief executive officer of Microsoft in January 2000, he assured all that he intended to remain a force in the company—primarily as the organization's lead hunter of leading-edge technologies. For Microsoft in its current incarnation, that means Gates will be spending time looking for and buying up companies that can move Microsoft into new markets.[4]

And how does the software giant go about making these strategic acquisitions? With cash, that's how.

Microsoft holds about $19 billion in cash, and the most important advantage of cash as an asset is its easy convertibility to other kinds of assets. You can move fast with cash.

In years past, Microsoft has done its share of acquisitions, but they

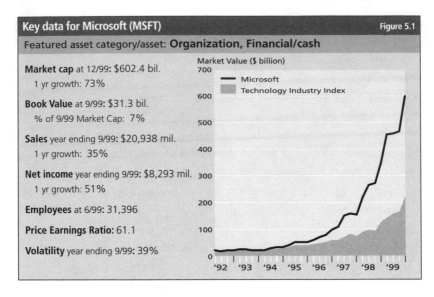

Key data for Microsoft (MSFT)   Figure 5.1

Featured asset category/asset: **Organization, Financial/cash**

Market cap at 12/99: $602.4 bil.
  1 yr growth: 73%

Book Value at 9/99: $31.3 bil.
  % of 9/99 Market Cap: 7%

Sales year ending 9/99: $20,938 mil.
  1 yr growth: 35%

Net income year ending 9/99: $8,293 mil.
  1 yr growth: 51%

Employees at 6/99: 31,396

Price Earnings Ratio: 61.1

Volatility year ending 9/99: 39%

Market Value ($ billion)
— Microsoft
■ Technology Industry Index

'92 '93 '94 '95 '96 '97 '98 '99

were mainly intended to support its own computer software research. Now, determined to move out from that base, the company is taking the fast track of cash acquisitions. Given the rapid pace of innovation these days, many other organizations have been going the same route.

In addition, Microsoft has been making some major cash investments in technology-rich organizations, including Apple Computer, Inc., Nextel Communications, Inc., and Akamai Technologies Inc. In 1999, for example, Microsoft reported 90 investments—71 equity investments, 14 acquisitions, and five joint ventures—totaling almost $10 billion. These transactions ranged from a $5 billion equity investment in AT&T to the smaller acquisition of CompareNet Inc., a comparison-shopping service on the Internet.

Investment, generally speaking, whether with Microsoft's high-flying stock or with its rich cash cache, has an incubation period before pay-off. The pay-off on an acquisition is more immediate, assuming of course that you made the right call to begin with.

Most of Microsoft's acquisitions have been in the communications arena, clearly a strategic target for the software maker. Bill Gates is determined to buy the technology that will keep his company on top, and the major carrot he can dangle in front of the companies he wants to buy is that most liquid of financial assets, cash.

Q. How do we define receivables?

We define receivables as claims a business expects to collect from its customers and others, usually arising from the sale of goods, provision of services, or advancement of funds. This amount—a current asset or short-term asset, according to standard accounting and reporting conventions—is listed on a company's balance sheet.

The receivables figure is based on the amount of money a company is owed by its customers. But, promises notwithstanding, the check doesn't always find its way into the mail, so the amount recorded on the balance sheet also reflects a sum set aside for "doubtful accounts" that probably won't be collected.

Q: Who is creating value with receivables?
A: Dell Computer Corporation.

How does Dell do it? It makes the most of its cash-conversion cycle—that is, the elapsed time between the day the company must pay its component suppliers and the day it finally receives customer payment.

For other computer manufacturers, the cash-conversion cycle may add up to weeks or even months. Not at Dell. By avoiding retailers and selling directly to customers, Dell typically gets paid four days before it must send a check to suppliers—for a cash-conversion cycle of minus four days.

That rapid (and virtually unheard of) turnaround was vital to Dell's ability to generate cash. Dell produced $2.4 billion in cash from operations in the company's 1999 fiscal year. It was money that Dell used to invest in other assets and finance internal growth.

In other words, Dell is using cash to get the most out of its entire asset portfolio. And it is all made possible by Dell's "Be Direct" business model, which eliminates distributors and links suppliers and customers.

Q. How do we define an investment?

As you might expect, we define investments as common stocks, bonds, and other financial instruments. In this era of the day trader, individual investors receive much media attention. But another type of investor, a corporate investor, can reap significant returns and create value by investing in the financial instruments of other businesses.

Sometimes one company invests in another to gain control of it. Our interest, however, is in minority investments that can create value over the long term. Like an individual investor, a company puts its money into the securities of another company or joint venture because it sees the promise of making even more money.

Q: Who is creating value with investments?
A: Lucent Technologies Inc.

When Lucent Technologies Inc. was created in 1996, its parent, AT&T Corporation, spun off not only its manufacturing operations but also the fabled Bell Laboratories division.[5]

Bell, the creator of countless innovations, perhaps most notably the transistor, does most of the in-house research and development for Lucent's diverse mix of products, including a wide range of public and private communication networks. The Bell division still receives an average of three new patents a day.

They don't come cheap, though. In 1997 and 1998, Bell Labs con-

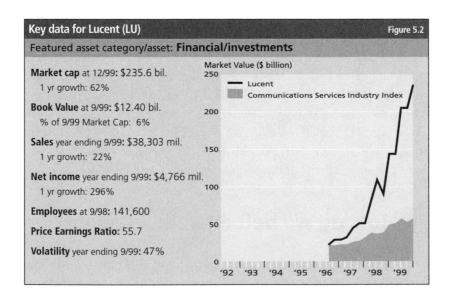

Key data for Lucent (LU)   Figure 5.2

Featured asset category/asset: **Financial/investments**

Market Value ($ billion)

Market cap at 12/99: $235.6 bil.
  1 yr growth: 62%

Book Value at 9/99: $12.40 bil.
  % of 9/99 Market Cap: 6%

Sales year ending 9/99: $38,303 mil.
  1 yr growth: 22%

Net income year ending 9/99: $4,766 mil.
  1 yr growth: 296%

Employees at 9/98: 141,600

Price Earnings Ratio: 55.7

Volatility year ending 9/99: 47%

— Lucent
  Communications Services Industry Index

'92 '93 '94 '95 '96 '97 '98 '99

sumed 11 percent of Lucent's operating budget. But Lucent, which is based in Murray Hill, New Jersey, has found a way to ease the expense of research at Bell Labs while also enhancing innovation. It has created a $100 million venture capital fund called Lucent Venture Partners.

The fund invests in small companies at work on emerging technologies (such as data networking, semiconductors, and communications software) that might be more expensive for Bell Labs to tackle internally. These companies not only provide Lucent with direct access to the newest technologies, but are expected to appreciate in value.

Investors' faith in Lucent was evident from the moment it floated what became the biggest initial public offering in history. Its market capitalization stood at $235.6 billion at the beginning of the year 2000 (versus $226.7 billion for its former parent). Through third quarter of 1999, Lucent's revenues topped $38.3 billion (up 22 percent) and net income totaled $4.8 billion (up a whopping 296 percent) as shown in Figure 5.2.

ⓠ How do we define debt?

We define debt as money owed to an outside party.

There are many sources of debt—from the ubiquitous credit-card variety to more esoteric vehicles like derivatives that have sprung up in recent years. But, in general, we are concerned with debt instruments such as bonds and term loans that a company uses to obtain capital— and create value.

Let's begin our analysis with a look at the simple economics of raising debt. Companies typically raise debt to invest cash in assets that generate a return exceeding the interest cost. The obligation to repay the amount borrowed is clearly not an asset. However, in a broader view, the ability to issue debt is an asset. It gives a company access to liquidity, which, in turn, enables it to create value from investing in other assets. The credit that companies take from their suppliers serves the same purpose.

Q: Who is creating value with debt?

A: Amazon.com, Inc.

Amazon.com, the virtual bookseller whose earth-bound headquarters are in Seattle, Washington, was among the first of the sizzling-hot Internet companies to offer a glimpse of how the Internet might transform retailing.[6]

The company, which bills itself as the earth's biggest bookstore but also sells music, videos, toys, electronics, software, and home improvement items, generated sales of $1.2 billion through the third quarter of 1999—a 188 percent increase from the year before. And the upward trend will be fueled by Amazon's pioneering of zShops, which create an on-line market for specialty goods.

So how is the on-line retailer financing its growth and generating wealth? With debt.

At the end of 1998, the company floated the first-ever high-yield issue by an Internet company (it totaled $326 million). Then, a few weeks later, it turned around and raised another $1.25 billion with an offering of convertible bonds.

The high-yield bonds are particularly interesting in that they give Amazon a five-year grace period before it has to make any payments. That fits nicely with expectations that this global e-tailer—which does

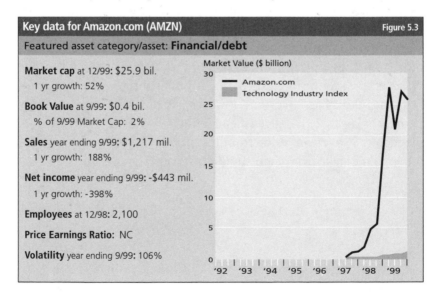

Key data for Amazon.com (AMZN)   Figure 5.3

Featured asset category/asset: **Financial/debt**

Market cap at 12/99: $25.9 bil.
  1 yr growth: 52%

Book Value at 9/99: $0.4 bil.
  % of 9/99 Market Cap: 2%

Sales year ending 9/99: $1,217 mil.
  1 yr growth: 188%

Net income year ending 9/99: -$443 mil.
  1 yr growth: -398%

Employees at 12/98: 2,100

Price Earnings Ratio: NC

Volatility year ending 9/99: 106%

Market Value ($ billion)

— Amazon.com
  Technology Industry Index

'92 '93 '94 '95 '96 '97 '98 '99

business in every one of the 50 states as well as some 150 other countries—will start making money early in this decade.

In the meantime, investors drove up the market capitalization of Amazon to $25.9 billion by the end of 1999, more than 60 times book value. (See Figure 5.3.)

Q How do we define equity?

We define equity as an ownership interest in the residual assets of an entity that remain after liabilities are deducted. In accounting terms, equity isn't an asset. However, just as with debt, we define the ability to raise equity by issuing stock as a key asset.

To acquire the funds needed to get a business off the ground or to expand a small business into a larger one, a company is usually forced to sell pieces of itself to an interested group of investors. Those transactions find their way onto a company's balance sheet as owner's equity (in the case of an unincorporated business) or as shareholders' equity (if the business is a corporation).

The role of equity is fundamental to Value Dynamics—and to risk management. Remember our second characteristic of value creation in the New Economy: Risk and opportunity are inseparable. In a world with no risk or uncertainty, little equity is required.

But today, in a time of rapid change and new ways to create value, many companies must rely on building equity in the financial markets. In short, the equity markets allow them to spread risk over many investors and generate a form of currency (stock) to be used for growth.

Said differently, whenever there is certainty, there is a reduced need for equity. In the New Economy, there is a significant need for equity, lots of it, because businesses are making big bets, and the market doesn't know whether they will pay off. Ask anyone who buys stock in Internet start-ups if they are certain of the valuations that discount decades—and in some cases centuries—of future earnings or cash flows.

Q: Who is creating value with equity?
A: Cisco Systems, Inc.

Back in the early 1980s, Leonard Bosack and Sandy Lerner were a husband-and-wife team of professors at Stanford University—he in the computer sciences department, she in the business school. Together they invented the so-called multiprotocol router, a device that allowed them to connect their previously incompatible computer networks at Stanford. The invention changed the world for all of us.[7]

By making it possible for millions of interconnected computer networks around the globe to exchange digitized data, the router gave birth to the Internet and then to a new Fortune 500 company, Cisco Systems, Inc., based in San Jose, California.

Bosack and Lerner, who founded Cisco in 1984, soon discovered that their router was in great demand. By 1993 the company had sold 124,000 routers and controlled 85 percent of the router market.

The future was not all rosy, however. Competitors were developing alternative routers, and new kinds of networking relay devices and switches were appearing with increasing frequency.

Customers became confused and unhappy about the high cost of building and keeping up-to-date a network of devices supplied by multiple vendors. To John T. Chambers, Cisco's president and chief executive

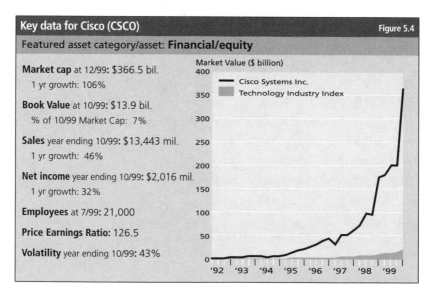

Key data for Cisco (CSCO) — Figure 5.4

Featured asset category/asset: **Financial/equity**

Market cap at 12/99: $366.5 bil.
 1 yr growth: 106%

Book Value at 10/99: $13.9 bil.
 % of 10/99 Market Cap: 7%

Sales year ending 10/99: $13,443 mil.
 1 yr growth: 46%

Net income year ending 10/99: $2,016 mil.
 1 yr growth: 32%

Employees at 7/99: 21,000

Price Earnings Ratio: 126.5

Volatility year ending 10/99: 43%

officer, the unhappiness and confusion spelled opportunity.

"Our customers told us that each vendor they took on added to the total cost of building the network," Chambers told Fortune. "For each dollar they would spend on networking hardware and software, they would spend $3 to $4 integrating them and administering them. Worse, when there was a problem, finger-pointing occurred. And more often than not, they would get five different answers from five different suppliers."

The solution, Chambers decided, was to transform Cisco into a full-service provider. But if Cisco wanted the requisite talent and technology,

> ## Cisco's stock price grew 124,825 percent in the last decade. And management used the ability to raise equity to finance growth.

it had to go shopping for the hot technology companies that were creating the bells and whistles. The question was, where would the money come from?

The company's leaders found their answer in Cisco's stock price—in other words, its equity asset. They used the company's ability to raise equity to finance growth.

After going public in 1990, Cisco's market capitalization grew to $6.6 billion by summer 1993. The company decided to make the most of its stock performance and attract the needed talent by offering to buy target companies with a piece of the rock—shares of Cisco itself—rather than cash.

Its first offer, in August 1993, involved a $90-million deal for Crescendo Communications, a maker of relatively simple devices called hubs which are used to link small work groups in local networks. By 1999 Cisco had traded shares of its high-flying stock for some 30 technology companies.

The skills and experience acquired in these transactions have enabled Cisco to give its customers full-service, end-to-end communications products. Along the way, the company has left its competitors in the dust. Annual revenues had risen to $13.4 billion through the third quarter of 1999, while net income was at $2 billion. (See Figure 5.4.)

And how do investors view Cisco's performance? Market capitalization stood at $366.5 billion by the end of 1999, 26 times its book value.

What made all this possible was Cisco's decision to use its stock to create a product and service offering that would increase customer spending and loyalty. Rising investor confidence and corporate valuation followed in turn.

▶ What's next?

In the next chapter, we explore the important category of employee and supplier assets.

We look first at Pfizer, Inc., maker of Viagra, the attention-grabbing drug that hit the market in April of 1998. By effectively using its huge sales force, Pfizer has capitalized on Viagra and a host of other pharmaceuticals.

Ask Yourself:

- Think of your company's different financial assets. Are you effectively managing these assets to create value for the business?

- How does your company's mix of financial assets contribute to its business model? Consider cash, receivables, investments, debt, and equity as sources of value creation.

- Do the case studies in this chapter suggest ways your company might change the way it manages its financial assets to create value?

- How do your competitors gain competitive advantage in the ways they maximize their financial assets?

- What are your industry's best practices for managing financial assets?

❑

6

Who is Creating Value with Employee and Supplier Assets?

"People are innately curious and, as social animals, are naturally motivated to interact and learn from one another."

—Sumantra Ghoshal and Christopher Bartlett[1]

When William C. Steere, Jr., became chief executive officer of New York-based Pfizer, Inc., in 1991, he had already spent 32 years with the pharmaceutical maker. Steere had worked his way up through the marketing ranks and was a true believer in the necessity of a large, down-in-the-trenches sales force. Unless physicians were personally contacted and educated about new, breakthrough drugs, he argued, they weren't likely to order them.

Prevailing wisdom held otherwise. The experts claimed that large sales teams were no longer needed and that pharmaceutical companies should purchase or contract with outside drug distributors to handle the lion's share of the job. The new chief didn't buy it.

Although Pfizer's sales force was already sizable and well regarded in the industry, Steere enlarged it, hiring and training top-flight talent. Cowen & Co., of Boston, estimates that Pfizer's sales staff now numbers 14,500, which makes it larger than that of Merck & Company, Inc., the giant of the industry.

And what about those experts who disputed Steere's convictions? Today they hail his wisdom.

Annual revenues were up 22 percent ($15.6 billion through the third quarter of 1999) and net income was at $2.9 billion. And investors have shown their approval by paying 55 times earnings for Pfizer stock. The company's market capitalization stood at $125.6 billion on January 1, 2000.

By making the most of Pfizer's sales force—which falls into the category of employee and supplier assets—Steere prepared the company to capitalize on its major new discoveries. What's more, he paved the way for Pfizer to take a leading role in the new era of so-called collaborative marketing.

In this chapter, we describe employee and supplier assets and show how businesses around the globe—such as the former Chrysler Corporation, USAA, and Virgin Group Ltd.—are using them to create value.

These assets encompass an organization's employees and its inbound supply chain. The category also includes partners. Each of these brings or supplies elements important to producing products and services. We examine each in turn, but we start with the backbone of any business, its employees.

Q. How do we define an employee?

"People," Howard Schultz, chairman and chief executive officer of Starbucks Corporation, once noted, "aren't a line item." But they are assets. Specifically, they are employee assets (sometimes referred to as human capital).

Virtually everyone at every level of an organization who works for financial compensation counts as an employee asset. Our definition encompasses full-time employees, part-time employees, independent contractors, even contingent workers. The value of employee assets lies in their skills, knowledge, experience, and attitudes and is enhanced by an organization's ability to hire, train, motivate, and retain the best people.

Q: Who is creating value with employees?
A: USAA.

General Wilson Cooney, former president of the property and casualty insurance group, USAA, was monitoring the phones at its San Antonio, Texas, headquarters one day when he happened to catch a conversation between a 24-year-old female service representative and an 81-year-old female customer.

"I need some help, but I'm not sure what with," the customer began, and that seemed true enough as she rambled on. Eventually, she explained her confusion: "I just lost my husband three weeks ago and I

> ## USAA's success grows out of its intimate understanding of and connection with its customers, who number 3.3 million.

don't know what to do." She had seen some insurance papers around the house, but had no idea what to do about them.

After offering condolences, the service representative suggested that the customer gather the papers together. The customer warned it might take a while—and it did. In fact, the call lasted 65 minutes. But by the time it ended, the service representative had resolved all the woman's problems with her auto, life, and estate policies.

"I just want to tell you this is the nicest thing that's happened to me in three weeks," the customer said. She sent the representative flowers.

"Those are the kinds of things that go on every day," Bill Cooney says, and, by all accounts, he was not exaggerating.[2]

For more than 77 years, USAA has focused first and foremost on achieving the best customer service in its industry, and it has succeeded: Ninety-eight percent of its customer base is in the top 40 percent for customer satisfaction; 98 percent of its members renew their policies each year. The secret, as Cooney makes clear, is in the interface between USAA's people and its customers. The company's skill at maximizing its employee assets is legendary.

The privately held company manages more than $56.5 billion in assets and is recognized as a leader in the financial services industry. In 1998, it earned $980 million on revenues of $7.7 billion.

USAA's success grows out of its intimate understanding of and connection with its customer-members, who number 3.3 million present or former military personnel and their families. It maintains real-time records of each customer transaction and makes the records instantly available to customer representatives on the phone or in the field. In other words, by using technology to furnish employees with up-to-the-minute information, the company makes the most of its employee assets and consequently provides greater value to customers.

At the same time, the company insists that employees be, as Cooney puts it, "passionate about serving people." Many of its 22,400 employees have special qualifications for empathizing with the uprooting, dangers, and other vicissitudes that characterize military life—they have been there themselves.

To make sure the right people are interacting with customers, USAA requires new employees to spend at least 10 weeks in training. One set of course names suggests the importance the company places on relationships with customers: "Conflict Resolution," "Relationship Management," "Complaint Handling," "Satisfaction Measurement," and "Needs Analysis."

Weeks are spent in concentrated technical training too, so that newcomers can properly benefit from the company's elaborate computer systems. And after formal training ends and they start answering the phones, new workers continue to be monitored and coached.

Another USAA program connects sales representatives directly with managers. The on-line system allows frontline workers to give managers feedback on their work lives and share their ideas for improving operations.

The leaders of USAA want to know what their employees are thinking and feeling. That kind of knowledge is useful when you want to instill in employees the attitudes that make for a service-first company.

The company's investment in employees thus takes many forms. USAA knows that it isn't enough to employ good people. To create

A USAA program connects sales people with managers on-line, allowing frontline workers to share ideas for improving operations.

value, employees must be properly trained, equipped, directed, and motivated. USAA provides a best-practice standard in this area.

Looking at USAA through the Value Dynamics lens, we see a company that has designed a business model that combines tangible and intangible assets, buttressed by the use of new and old technologies, to meet its goals. In the process, it has come up with a win-win situation for the company as a whole, including customers and employees.

ⓠ How do we define a supplier?

We define a supplier as anyone who furnishes materials, products, or services. If you want to know how important suppliers are, ask Charles H. Fine, a professor at the Sloan School of Management at the Massachusetts Institute of Technology.[3] He tells the story about how, in 1997, a group of managers at what was then Chrysler Corporation (the company has since merged with Daimler-Benz to become Daimler-Chrysler AG) set about exploring the capabilities of the company's suppliers. They focused on a portion of the supply chain of the Jeep Grand Cherokee, starting with the V-8 engine and moving on to a valve lifter.

One company, it turned out, provided the raw casting for the valve lifter. Another was the sole source of the foundry clay used to make the casting.

To the managers' dismay, they learned that the owner of the clay company was planning to abandon the foundry business and start making kitty litter. Without the clay supplier, Chrysler faced a severe shortage of foundry clay, which would halt the manufacture of raw castings, valve lifters, and eventually Grand Cherokee engines.

Before undertaking this exercise, Chrysler executives didn't even know the clay supplier existed. Nor did the clay company's owner know that his product was critical to Chrysler. Suddenly the executives came calling, pleading with the owner to delay his move.

His answer: "OK, make it worth my while and I'll stay out of kitty litter." Chrysler made it worth his while.

Clearly companies are dependent upon their suppliers, as well as their suppliers' suppliers, and so on down the line. Identifying different supplier assets can pave the way for creating value or, as in Chrysler's case, become the lifesaver that keeps value from disappearing. Suppliers may also enhance the value of other assets, including employees and customers.

If a company's goal is to make the most of its supplier assets— that is, to bring new value out of a network of suppliers— three elements matter more than others. They are the capabilities of the suppliers, the strength of a company's relationship with them, and the way they interact with other assets in the portfolio to create corporate value.

Chrysler, as we shall see, has long experience in nurturing its supplier relationships. It is a track record that speaks for itself.

Q: Who is creating value with suppliers?

A: DaimlerChrysler AG.

Fifteen years ago, when the former Chrysler Corporation was still recovering from its brush with bankruptcy, the number three automaker in the United States came up with a new approach to suppliers—an approach partly modeled on the lean production system that had turned Japan's Toyota Auto Body Company Ltd., into the world's most efficient auto manufacturer.

Like its two Detroit rivals, Ford Motor Company and General Motors Corporation, Chrysler had always produced most car components in-house. Suppliers competed hard for the leavings, and the Big Three squeezed them for all they were worth.

Chrysler, its back to the wall, decided to rewrite the rules of supplier relationships. The company began outsourcing major parts and subsys-

Suppliers' ideas boost Chrysler profits hundreds of millions of dollars annually.

tems. It signed long-term contracts with individual suppliers. It brought them in on cost-cutting discussions and technological development, sharing the financial benefits achieved.

It worked.

To put it in our terms, Chrysler found new opportunity in its re-energized supplier asset because it paid attention to market signals that were pointing to a need for slimmed-down, more efficient operations.

One story offers a case in point: A metal-casting supplier suggested that Chrysler substitute a plastic part for the one that the supplier was making, even though it meant the supplier would lose a substantial chunk of business.

The change saved $4 per car, a huge sum in purchasing terms. The supplier was rewarded with other metal-casting business to make up the difference.

In this particular instance, Chrysler enhanced the value of its supplier assets by building a long-term relationship based on commonality of economic interest. Chrysler's strategy also uses financial assets to encourage supplier loyalty and thus create value.

Chrysler managers estimate that thousands of cost-reduction ideas submitted by its suppliers boost company profits by hundreds of millions of dollars each year. So Chrysler is using supplier assets to maximize the value of its entire asset portfolio.

DaimlerChrysler reported revenues of some $192 billion for 1998. Its market capitalization stood at $78.1 billion on January 1, 2000.[3]

ⓠ How do we define a partner?

In a simpler age, companies carved out their niches, the corners of the market where their competitive advantage could be sustained, and went about their business. An occasional predator might appear, intent on invading a company's turf or even swallowing it up, but they were few and far between.

Today the woods are full of predators—and they hail not only from your home country but from around the globe. As a result, the pace of

> **Companies are maximizing partner assets to protect their flanks, extend geographic reach, and start new businesses.**

business has accelerated markedly, and the dream of perpetual independence has given way to an era of new alliances and partnerships.

We define partners as parties associated as joint principals in a business venture. And we define joint ventures as contractual arrangements in which two or more partners undertake economic activity that is subject to joint control.

To prosper, companies are maximizing their partner assets to protect their flanks, to extend their geographic reach, to add to their product or service lines, and even—as in the case of Virgin Group Ltd.—to create whole new businesses.

Q: Who is creating value with partners?

A: Virgin Group Ltd.

Privately held Virgin Group Ltd., the travel, entertainment, and retailing conglomerate based in London, England, posts revenues of more than $5 billion annually, and its tentacles reach to every continent. More than 200 companies worldwide have been hatched in the Virgin incubator.

And what a diverse lot they are. The travel sector includes Virgin Atlantic and Virgin Express airlines, Virgin Holidays, Virgin Hotels, Virgin Trains, Virgin Limobike, and Virgin Limousines. Under the entertainment banner resides Virgin Radio, Virgin Publishing, and Virgin Cola, not to mention the more than 100 Virgin Megastores that can be found in major cities around the world.

There are also media companies, financial management firms, and a blimp business—all sporting the Virgin name. Throw in clothing, cosmetics, and health clubs, and it becomes apparent that absolutely nothing is off limits as far as Virgin's founder, chairman, and chief executive officer Richard Branson, is concerned.

Fearless and flamboyant, Branson's media stunts (he promoted the opening of his Virgin Bride business by posing for photographers in a lavish white silk bridal gown complete with veil and lace train) and around-the-world ballooning ventures sometimes overshadow the fact that he is a savvy businessman with no shortage of profitable ideas. He has also assembled a high-caliber executive team to help keep the burgeoning empire on solid ground.

Branson pursues an ingenious strategy that he calls "branded venture capital" to use partner assets to create value.[4] He has developed numerous joint ventures to which he contributes the Virgin name and his flair for public relations, relying on his partners to put up the capital—much as though Virgin were a franchise operation.

The approach has worked brilliantly. For example, Branson invested a mere $1,700 for a 50 percent share of Virgin Vie cosmetics. The remaining 50 percent went for $35 million, which was the sum raised by Virgin's partner, Victory Corporation, a small British company.

Branson got his start in business in the late 1960s, when he began a national student magazine. He was 16 years old. In 1970, at the age of

18, he launched Virgin Records, which went on to become Britain's largest independent label, featuring such mega-hit artists as the Rolling Stones and Phil Collins.

Forced to sell the record business in 1992 to raise cash to keep then-struggling start-up Virgin Air aloft, Branson vowed never to be at the mercy of bankers again. That's how his branded venture-capital strategy was born. It lets him get businesses off the ground with minimal personal investment.[5]

He typically starts small, which keeps him from draining a cash hoard that *BusinessWeek* put at $420 million in 1998. Branson claims his

> Virgin's ingenious strategy — "branded venture capital" — uses partner assets to create value.

companies throw off $250 million more in cash flow each year, with very little debt. Virgin Group had sales of $5 billion for the year ending October 1998, up 20 percent from the prior year.[6] And recently, the company sold 49 percent of Virgin Airlines to Singapore Airlines for several hundred million dollars.

Virgin Group, with its ever-expanding list of companies and 25,000 employees, has mastered the art of creating value with partners.

Q: Who else is creating value with partners?

A: Psion PLC.

For much of 1998, the stock of Psion PLC, London, England, was in the doldrums. Investors were nervous that little Psion's popular hand-held electronic organizers were vulnerable to attack from Microsoft Corporation and other electronics giants.[7]

Not waiting around to be bullied by the big boys, Psion decided to shore up its defenses by making friends with a pretty tough group of players all on its own. Finland's Nokia Corporation and Sweden's Ericsson AB, two of the top names in mobile phones, and America's Motorola, Inc., one of the world's most advanced electronics companies, joined forces with Psion in a venture called Symbian Ltd.

The joint venture seeks to develop Psion's operating system as the platform for a new generation of mobile communication devices, including mobile phones, palm-tops, and handheld Internet connectivity devices.

What was the reaction of the stock market? After languishing at the equivalent of about $3.30 a share before the deal was announced, Psion's stock had nearly tripled a week later—even though founder and chairman David E. Potter cautioned that earnings would initially be pulled down by costs associated with the alliance. And the stock continued to rise. A year later, Psion's stock was trading at around $16 a share.

▶ What's next?

In the chapter that follows, we begin by taking a look at how The Charles Schwab Corporation has surprised even itself by evolving from a small-potatoes discount broker into something strikingly similar to a full-service brokerage. How did Schwab do it? By making the most of its customer assets.

Ask Yourself:

- Think of your company's employee and supplier assets. Are you effectively managing these assets to create value?

- How does your company's mix of employees, suppliers, and partners contribute to its business model?

- Do the case studies in this chapter suggest any ways that your company might manage its employee and supplier assets more effectively?

- How does your company track and measure the value-creating contributions of employees, suppliers, and partners?

- What are the best practices in your industry when it comes to managing employee and supplier assets? How do your competitors gain advantage with their employee and supplier assets?

Who is Creating Value with Customer Assets?

"Customers do not want more choice. They want exactly what they want—when, where, and how they want it."

—B. Joseph Pine II, Don Peppers and Martha Rogers[1]

When The Charles Schwab Corporation opened its first office in 1971, the discount broker boasted a bare-bones mission: Give investors the opportunity to buy or sell whatever stocks they want at a price far below what full-service competitors charge.

Schwab wasn't in the business of advising clients or recommending stocks. An investor gave Schwab an order and never heard from the firm again.

Based on that simple formula, San Francisco-based Schwab—through its primary operating unit, Charles Schwab & Company, Inc.—amassed millions of customers. These independent-minded people opened accounts worth billions of dollars.

But in the 1990s, Schwab found itself dealing with a new breed of customer—people who wanted to be part of the bull market but knew little or nothing about the ways of Wall Street. Schwab responded by reinventing itself.

It began offering clients mountains of information as well as a variety of new services. In 1998, for example, Schwab made arrangements with Credit Suisse First Boston and Hambrecht & Quist to distribute their analyst reports to Schwab customers. Neither firm has retail brokers of its own.

Schwab, it seems, is starting to look a lot like those full-commission brokerages it disavowed in days of yore. "Where we're going," Daniel O. Leemon, chief strategy officer for Schwab, told *BusinessWeek*, "is the direction in which our customers are leading us."[2]

Along the way, Schwab has made the most of its clients. That is, it is using its customer assets to gain competitive advantage, cut costs, and even enter entirely new businesses—like the management of initial public offerings (IPOs). The result—new value.

On December 4, 1998, Schwab announced that it would serve as co-manager of an IPO for Select Comfort Corporation, a Minneapolis, Minnesota, manufacturer of air mattresses. Select Comfort was selling

> ## Schwab added $100 billion in customer assets in the last two months of 1999 alone.

4 million shares at $17 each. Although Schwab had been offering shares of IPOs to customers for a year, this was its first foray into managing an IPO—a role heretofore reserved for the likes of Merrill Lynch & Company, Inc., or Morgan Stanley Dean Witter & Company.

Its participation in IPO management means Schwab has access to more shares than it would as an outsider. It also means the company can participate in a remunerative corner of the market previously claimed exclusively by investment bankers.

The lead manager of the Select Comfort IPO, Hambrecht & Quist, welcomed Schwab because the discounter is such a giant in its own right.

Schwab mined information about its accounts to identify some 250,000 customers of both Schwab and Select Comfort. These customers received postcards from Schwab alerting them to the mattress maker's public offering.

Schwab is particularly keen to capitalize on its Internet clients, who number more than 3 million. It can plumb personal profiles and portfolios of individual customers, looking for a match with a particular upcoming IPO. It might alert a builder, for example, to an IPO of a home-improvement retailer.

By providing its Internet customers with ever-increasing content, Schwab is adding to the "stickiness" of its Web site. In other words, it is reducing the likelihood that users will go to other sites for information.

In the beginning, one of Schwab's advantages as a discount broker was the money it saved on employees. When the company did little more than execute trades, it didn't need training programs—not to mention huge payrolls or employee benefits. But the move toward full service altered that equation, and payroll costs escalated.

What did Schwab do? It began a campaign to convince clients to serve themselves. It talked millions of its customers into doing what Schwab employees had been doing for them.

Telephone callers were persuaded to use automated lines and www.schwab.com for routine business. Customers who used Schwab's 337 branch offices were urged to go on-line for a speedier response to their requests for individual stock quotes and to make trades. Schwab branches even offered customers training in how to use the Internet.

As a result, Schwab cut its payroll for ordertakers and used the savings to bring in a different type of branch-office worker—employees who are trained to advise customers on investment needs.

Today, almost half of Schwab's accounts are on-line, and about 60 percent of new customers do business with schwab.com. It dominates the on-line trading market, chalking up more than $10 billion in securities transactions each week.

The company has amassed value by connecting its customers via three channels—branch offices, telephone service, and the Internet—to a variety of other assets, including the products and services of other financial services firms. Using these channels has also allowed Schwab to scale its offerings for distribution to large numbers of customers. It

> ## Schwab dominates the on-line trading market, chalking up more than $10 billion in securities transactions each week.

boasts more than 6.4 million customers, with more than $700 billion of assets in Schwab accounts. Indeed, Schwab added $100 billion in customer assets in the last two months of 1999 alone. Some 236,000 trades were made on average each day in December of that year.

Schwab is a prime example of a company that is creating value with its customer assets. In our parlance, the term customer asset applies to more than just the end user of a product or service. It also includes a company's channels and affiliates, because each is an essential link in the chain that runs from originator of a good or service to its ultimate consumer.

This chapter explores each asset in turn, but our first concern is for the individual or organization that makes it all possible—the customer.

Q. How do we define a customer?

It goes without saying that customers, whom we define as the buyers of a product or service, are crucial to a business. No one knew that better than Samuel Moore Walton, the late and legendary founder, chairman, and chief executive officer of giant Wal-Mart Stores, Inc., who once declared: "We exist to provide value to our customers. . . . Nothing happens until a customer walks into a store with a purpose, buys something, and walks out."

Or as Lawrence A. Bossidy, former chairman and chief executive officer of AlliedSignal, Inc., the Morristown, New Jersey-based maker of aerospace, automotive, and engineered materials products, told the Economic Club of Washington: "It's not management who decides how many people are on the payroll. It's customers. . . . Without a growing roster of satisfied customers, we can all turn out the lights and go home."[3]

To make the most of customer assets, winning businesses seek to lock in customers, to establish mutually beneficial and lasting relationships. In other words, they seek to have better quality relationships that increase the size and longevity of the customer asset.

Q: Who is creating value with customers?
A: Gap Inc.

Gap Inc. and its brands are everywhere, and so are its customers. Because of The Gap's unusual presence and reach, it has been a powerhouse in amassing customer assets. But it doesn't rely solely on storefronts to attract its hordes of shoppers, even though it is opening up new outlets at the rate of one a day.

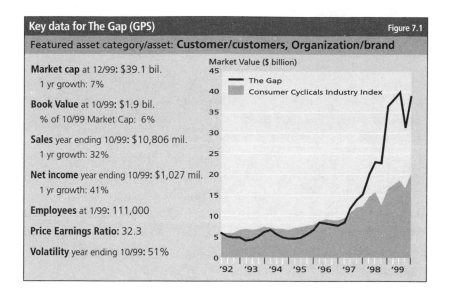

Key data for The Gap (GPS)   Figure 7.1

Featured asset category/asset: **Customer/customers, Organization/brand**

Market cap at 12/99: $39.1 bil.
  1 yr growth: 7%

Book Value at 10/99: $1.9 bil.
  % of 10/99 Market Cap: 6%

Sales year ending 10/99: $10,806 mil.
  1 yr growth: 32%

Net income year ending 10/99: $1,027 mil.
  1 yr growth: 41%

Employees at 1/99: 111,000

Price Earnings Ratio: 32.3

Volatility year ending 10/99: 51%

Market Value ($ billion)

The Gap
Consumer Cyclicals Industry Index

'92 '93 '94 '95 '96 '97 '98 '99

Under the leadership of president and chief executive officer Mickey Drexler, Gap Inc. also goes to customers through a variety of other channels of distribution—direct mail, telephone sales, and one of the most successful e-commerce sites in retail, which cross-promotes with the traditional stores. "Measure your khakis," the Web site announces.

Viewed from the perspective of Value Dynamics, it is clear that The Gap excels at using both customer and supplier assets in combination with physical assets (storefronts) and new and old technology (e-commerce and telephone sales). It is acquiring new customers at a rapid clip with trend-setting and highly targeted advertising. This, after all, is the company that got the New York Stock Exchange to take its first "casual Friday"—and it offered the clothes with which to do it.

The company has also been successful at differentiating its marketing strategies and product offerings by forming other chains (Banana Republic and Old Navy) and adding line extensions.

Gap Inc. seems to have the right idea when it comes to leveraging customers to create value. Annual revenue reached $10.8 billion through the third quarter of 1999, up 32 percent from the prior year, while net income amounted to $1 billion, up 41 percent. Investors had bestowed a market capitalization of $39.1 billion through January 1, 2000—more than 20 times the clothing chain's book value.

(Q) How do we define a channel?

A channel is critical to moving merchandise or services from a supplier to a consumer or end user. Thus channel assets are a key part of any company's go-to-market model.

Channel companies that actually take title to a product and then eventually sell it to someone else are called merchant middlemen. Wholesalers and retailers fall into this category.

In the New Economy, channels offer access to bigger audiences and markets than ever before. The Internet, for example, is a channel par excellence. Channels can enable scalability and enhance all the other assets in a portfolio. Not all channel strategies involve the Internet, however, as our next case study shows.

Q: Who is creating value with channel assets?
A: Duracell, Inc.

Duracell, Inc., of Bethel, Connecticut, has a single-minded focus: It sells batteries—3 billion every year.

They come in a variety of sizes, shapes, and materials—from the old standard, the alkaline battery, to the newer lithium ion and nickel metal hydride types. In a modern-day version of the tortoise and the hare, Duracell's Copper Top outruns the Energizer Bunny as the number one alkaline battery worldwide.

But the battery, as good as it is, isn't the point of our story. What has helped power Duracell to the head of the pack is its use of channel assets.

Duracell batteries are available as stand-alone products in retail stores throughout the world, of course. But Duracell's greater strength is behind the scenes, so to speak, in the host of product offerings that are battery-run.

The mother photographing her children with a 35mm camera or the father using a camcorder to film his high-school hurdler is likely to be holding a piece of equipment powered by a Duracell battery. Look inside a hearing aid, a home security system, a television remote control, a cellular phone, or a handheld computer game and you are likely to encounter the Duracell brand name.

The company's channel assets are the products and services developed by other companies. And Duracell continues to expand its market share by devising new ways to support those offerings. Its new Ultra

> ## In the New Economy, channels can offer access to vast audiences and more markets than ever before. Duracell knows how.

alkaline battery, for example, increases the operating life of high technology tools. With the help of a $60 million promotional campaign, Ultra has captured about 50 percent market share in the United States. On another front, Duracell is expanding its operations and product line by buying top battery brands overseas and introducing their technologically superior batteries.

The company's financials reflect its success with channel assets. Duracell—which merged with the Gillette Company in 1996—generated $2.6 billion in revenues, an increase of 4 percent for 1998.[4]

Q How do we define an affiliate?

An accountant would apply a strict set of ownership standards before labeling a business as an affiliate. But we prefer to think of affiliates in relational terms. We define them as closely associated organizations.

For example, SAirGroup, based in Zurich, Switzerland, maintains an affiliation with a number of airlines throughout Europe, including Sabena, TAP Air Portugal, Turkish Airlines, and French AOM, among others. In what SAirGroup describes as "a close collaboration," the alliance partners share information and customers. They coordinate timetables and maintain standardized fares that make it easy to book passengers on one another's flights. Revenues on joint routes are shared according to agreed-upon formulas.

Q: Who is creating value with affiliates?

A: Autobytel.com, Inc.

For anyone who hates haggling over the price of a car—or who just hates car shopping—Autobytel.com, Inc. is a real boon.

Think of Autobytel as an on-line matchmaking service for car buyers and car dealerships. Like any good matchmaker, it is making both parties happy by sending only customers who are ready to buy to dealers who are able to provide exactly what the customer wants—at an agreed-upon, no-haggle price.

It is a match made in cyber-heaven.

Based in Irvine, California, the company was founded in 1995 by a former car dealer, Peter Ellis. Autobytel now works with nearly 2,900 North American auto retailers, which pay monthly fees to be affiliated with its network. Why? Because Autobytel generates in excess of $1.6 million an hour in car sales. J. D. Powers reports that Autobytel is the largest auto e-tailer, accounting for fully 45 percent of all new vehicles sold over the Internet.

When prospective car buyers log on to www.autobytel.com, they can check out everything from a particular car's features, to critics' reviews, to prices and available rebates, to financing—even insurance. Or the cus-

> **Affiliates can be powerful ways to leverage value. Autobytel leads on-line, uniting auto buyers and sellers.**

tomer in a hurry simply keys in a price range and desired features, where-upon Autobytel quickly calls up vehicles that match the customer's needs.

Customers interested in buying a particular vehicle click on their choice and indicate when they wish to purchase it. An image of the model appears on the screen with a checklist of available options.

As customers select different options, the dealer invoice and the man-ufacturer's suggested retail price changes. Eventually, the customized pur-chase request produces what amounts to an on-line window sticker that is ready for direct routing to one of Autobytel's affiliate dealerships.

The affiliate dealer is required to contact the customer within 24 hours and offer a competitive, no-haggle quote. Autobytel managers hope to have as many as 3,500 dealerships in their North American network of affiliates through the year 2000. "We'll grow as fast as we can find dealers who have bought into the process and are ready to deliver our customers the service they want," president and chief executive officer Mark W. Lorimer explains.

Autobytel reported sales of $35.2 million through the third quarter of 1999 and a net loss of $22.3 million. The market value of the company was at $300 million on January 1, 2000. Autobytel.com is rewriting the script on how to create value with affiliates, while it invests heavily as a new dot.com in developing and marketing services.[5]

▶ What's next?

Whether it is Schwab accessing its bank of some 6.4 million clients or Autobytel working with affiliates, the message is clear: Customer assets are being used to create enormous value across a range of industries.

Now we turn to our last value-creating category, organization assets. These assets are fundamental to allocation of a company's resources, as our examples will illustrate.

The organization segment comprises a list headed—fittingly, we think—by leadership assets. After all, it is the management team that must build an asset portfolio capable of delivering value to a company's stakeholders.

Ask Yourself:

- Think of your company's customer assets. Is your organization effectively managing these assets to create value?

- How does your company's mix of customer assets—including customers, channels, and affiliates—contribute to value?

- Do the case studies in this chapter give you any ideas for managing your company's customer assets more effectively?

- How does your company track and measure the value-creating contributions of its customers? Its channels? Its affiliates?

- What are the best practices in your industry when it comes to managing customer assets? How do your competitors gain advantage with their customer assets?

Who is Creating Value with Organization Assets?

"The range of
new economic
combinations
is immense and
the choice of
one rather than
another is, in
the last analysis,
an exercise in
human, or
entrepreneurial,
judgment."

—R. H. Campbell and R.G. Wilson.[1]

"Being a hero," the wise and witty Will Rogers once said, "is about the shortest-lived profession on earth."[2] Steven P. Jobs, the once and interim chief executive officer of Apple Computer, Inc., based in Cupertino, California, knows that better than most.

As co-founder of Apple in 1976, and co-designer of the Apple II personal computer, Jobs was hailed as both a business visionary and an engineering wizard. In 1984 he reached his pinnacle as hero, launching the elegant Apple Macintosh, which transformed personal-computing.[3]

The next year he was history—forced out, as *Forbes* magazine once put it, by "a treacherous Pepsi pusher." (Then president and chief executive officer John Sculley, a former PepsiCo, Inc., executive, had been handpicked by Jobs to bring management experience to Apple. After one too many missteps, Sculley himself was ousted by the board of directors in 1993.)

In the fall of 1998, Jobs was re-anointed as hero. Wearing his customary faded jeans and black turtleneck, he took to the stage of the Flint Center in Cupertino and told a crowd of journalists and analysts about his first year back at Apple.

In just 12 months—aided by the introduction of the stylish, low-cost iMac—he had turned a $1-billion loss into a $309-million profit.

If Will Rogers had it right—and he usually did—Jobs' hero status won't last forever. But this much can be said: His leadership has transformed Apple from a company seemingly doomed to oblivion to one with a strong claim to a future.

> ## Jobs is an asset whose wealth-generating power is reflected in Apple's turnaround—$100 invested on January 1, 1999 was worth $688 a year later.

Jobs is an asset whose wealth-generating power is reflected in Apple's earnings turnaround. It is also reflected in the company's market value. Apple's market capitalization on January 1, 2000 was $16.6 billion, after a meteoric climb through 1999. One hundred dollars invested in Apple on January 1, 1999 was worth $688 a year later.

There is something wrong with this picture, however. When you look at Apple's financial statements— or those of almost any other company, for that matter—you won't find leadership listed among the assets. As we have pointed out—and will continue to do throughout this book—traditional accounting ignores many intangible assets.

Value Dynamics includes leadership in an asset category we call organization. This category embraces both structural and intellectual assets. It therefore includes strategy, structure, culture and values, processes, systems, the capacity to innovate, brands, and proprietary knowledge. In Apple's case, all of these assets have been deployed in combination to create value.

In this chapter, we explore the entire panoply of organization assets, using a variety of business examples to illustrate the importance of these often overlooked treasures. Organization assets provide the glue that holds a company together. But more than that, they are crucial to galvanizing your organization to respond to the challenges of the New Economy.

Established companies often find it difficult to change their business models to create value because they neglect organization assets. They might make all the right moves to realign asset portfolios in terms of physical, financial, employee and supplier, and customer assets, only to become frustrated at the results (or lack of them). This is precisely why you must remember that your company is all of its assets, including the organization ones.

Every company should determine whether its organization assets still work for success in the New Economy. To put it another way, a company might have structures, processes, systems, culture, values, and knowledge, which it has developed and cherished over decades. But instead of holding the company together, the combination might no longer be the tie that binds. If that's the case, you will need to bid them farewell and invest in new ways of doing things. That task can be enormous. To succeed, the first thing you will need is the right sort of leadership to create a sense of challenge and urgency.

Ⓠ How do we define leadership?

We define leadership as the capacity to inspire, organize, lead, and manage the value-creation process.

Q: Who is creating value with leadership?
A: International Business Machines Corporation.

Louis V. Gerstner, Jr., began his stint at International Business Machines Corporation (IBM) on April Fool's Day, 1993. The first chairman and chief executive officer not to rise through the company's ranks, he came to IBM to rescue it.[4]

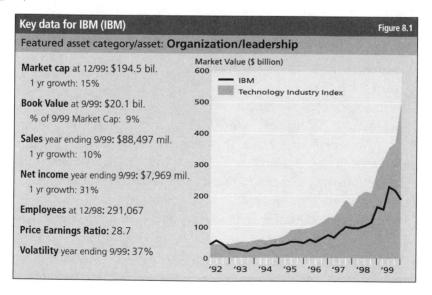

Key data for IBM (IBM)   Figure 8.1

Featured asset category/asset: **Organization/leadership**

Market cap at 12/99: $194.5 bil.
  1 yr growth: 15%

Book Value at 9/99: $20.1 bil.
  % of 9/99 Market Cap: 9%

Sales year ending 9/99: $88,497 mil.
  1 yr growth: 10%

Net income year ending 9/99: $7,969 mil.
  1 yr growth: 31%

Employees at 12/98: 291,067

Price Earnings Ratio: 28.7

Volatility year ending 9/99: 37%

Market Value ($ billion)

— IBM
▨ Technology Industry Index

'92 '93 '94 '95 '96 '97 '98 '99

And he made his mark quickly.

Shunning the course set by his predecessor, John Akers, Gerstner announced early on that he would not break up Big Blue. He did, however, cut the workforce, from 406,000 to 219,000 employees, and he took a $20 billion write-off.

He also changed IBM's traditional management-by-committee approach. These days, each manager has to speak for his or her own department, instead of allowing aides to present carefully crafted expositions.

Gerstner decided, too, that IBM would rebuild its personal-computer division and that it would focus on service. "This technology is hard stuff," he told *Fortune*. "What I really want is somebody to help me implement it." The chief went on to say that the company had to "reorient from a highly introspective view of the world to an obsession with the marketplace, meaning with both customers and competitors."

The company's first task— "to attack the critical problems," which Gerstner ticked off as "our lack of competitive cost structure, inefficiencies, unconsummated strategies that were destroying profits, and products that were not competitive."

The turnaround has been nothing short of spectacular. Whereas

> ## Gerstner calls market value the "ultimate measure" of performance. IBM's market cap rose more than six-fold under his leadership by year-end 1999.

IBM posted an $8.1 billion loss in 1993, six years later it reported net income of $8 billion on revenues of $88.5 billion (through the third quarter of 1999). (See Figure 8.1.)

As for market valuation, which Gerstner has called the "ultimate measure of our performance," that too has been enhanced by the power of his leadership. When Gerstner took over in 1993, IBM's market value was $29 billion. By January 1, 2000, it had risen to $194.5 billion, more than a six-fold increase.

By reputation, Gerstner is thorough, tough, hardheaded, forceful, brusque to the point of rudeness, ambitious, and unhampered by IBM traditions. When asked to describe his leadership style, he rounds out the profile with additional adjectives like intense, competitive, focused, and blunt.

Gerstner came to IBM with a known track record as an executive who understood and paid attention to customer needs. But more to the point, he helped IBM to effect what many established organizations cannot—that is, a change in business model and strategy that eventually permeates the entire organization.

What Gerstner isn't is a social animal. After a meeting is over, he leaves—no coffee, no lunch, no chitchat. Before he sees an executive, he demands a written statement that outlines the points to be discussed. No time is wasted on polite small talk.

One IBMer told *Fortune* that Gerstner "revels in complexity, and this is a five-dimensional chess game. We buy from competitors. We sell to the same competitors. We sue competitors. We've got complex relationships." Lou Gerstner has the sort of mind and leadership style that can sort out and disentangle such intricacies.

"We got lucky," Gerstner told shareholders at the 1997 annual meeting. "It's not often a company gets a second shot at [industry] leadership. But that's all it is, a shot. We still have to compete, we still have to execute." [5]

Ⓠ How do we define structure?

The structure of an organization is often represented by an organization chart. The concept is, of course, not new. Organization charts predate the onset of the Industrial Age. Similar diagrams—what the French call an organigramme—can, in fact, be found outlining the church hierarchy in medieval Spain.

It is easy to understand why organization charts have been around so long. Being able to visualize the structure of an organization is a useful tool for understanding how it works. And structural understanding can spark value creation.

Q: **Who is creating value with structure?**
A: **Johnson & Johnson.**

"Conventional thinking says that as you get bigger, you have to slow down," Ralph S. Larsen, chairman and chief executive officer of Johnson &

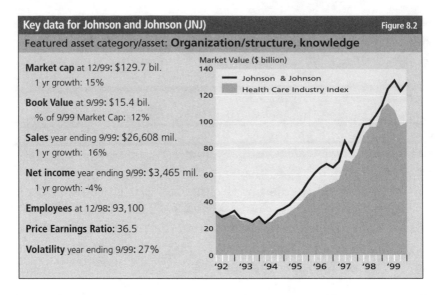

Key data for Johnson and Johnson (JNJ)   Figure 8.2

Featured asset category/asset: **Organization/structure, knowledge**

Market cap at 12/99: $129.7 bil.
  1 yr growth: 15%

Book Value at 9/99: $15.4 bil.
  % of 9/99 Market Cap: 12%

Sales year ending 9/99: $26,608 mil.
  1 yr growth: 16%

Net income year ending 9/99: $3,465 mil.
  1 yr growth: -4%

Employees at 12/98: 93,100

Price Earnings Ratio: 36.5

Volatility year ending 9/99: 27%

Market Value ($ billion)

— Johnson & Johnson
▓ Health Care Industry Index

'92 '93 '94 '95 '96 '97 '98 '99

Johnson, headquartered in New Brunswick, New Jersey, likes to say. He also frequently notes, "But . . . we have a formula for sustaining growth, and that formula . . . is our structure."[6]

J&J's structure is an asset that is unique among the Fortune 500. While its competitors maintain a small number of subsidiaries and operating companies, the world's largest health care products company juggles 33 lines of business and 188 operating companies in 52 countries.

Johnson & Johnson is amazingly decentralized, and it is this structure that enables the company to roll out innovation after innovation. New value follows: Products introduced within the last five years account for some 35 percent of J&J's annual revenues of more than $26 billion in three business segments (consumer, professional and pharmaceutical). Investment in research and development hit $2.6 billion in 1998.

On its face, that kind of structure and the myriad products it turns out might suggest disarray, but far from it. The various pieces of Johnson & Johnson operate in concert. Synergy occurs naturally. The people at the surgical-needle company, for example, share their patented metal-polishing technology with the people at the coronary-implant company. And on it goes.

Johnson & Johnson is among the most admired—and profitable—companies in the world, with net income of nearly $3.5 billion in the year ending the third quarter of 1999. The company's market value was $129.7 billion on January 1, 2000. (See Figure 8.2.)

Ⓠ How do we define processes?

Process is the language of business that everyone must understand before real improvements can take place. Processes encompass the actual work of an organization. That is, they are the series of operations, methods, actions, tasks, or functions leading to the creation of an end product or service.

They can also be a key source of new value.

The order-fulfillment process is an example. Order fulfillment starts when a customer's order is entered into a computer and the customer's credit rating is checked. Once the order is approved, it is scheduled for production. A shipping method is then chosen, and the finished product is packed and posted.

No single piece of the process is, by itself, of value to the company: You can't ship without the product in hand, and you can't have the product in hand without the order being scheduled into production. Rather, it is the order-fulfillment process as a whole, encompassing a series of interdependent actions, that creates value for the company.

It was the reengineering movement that started companies thinking about processes as value-creating assets. "We knew that companies could dramatically improve their efficiency and quality by focusing on customers and the processes that create value for them," says Michael Hammer, a Cambridge, Massachusetts, pioneer of the reengineering movement. "But we didn't realize that companies' processes would . . . come to be even more important than their products. We started out thinking that if we could improve their processes, we could help them compete better in their chosen markets. And now it turns out that processes are, in fact, determining the markets in which the companies compete." [7]

Q: Who is creating value with processes?
A: Pfizer, Inc.

Pharmaceutical maker Pfizer Inc. boasts perhaps the richest new-product pipeline in the drug business, with 16 medications in advanced development or registration and some 55 compounds in early develop-

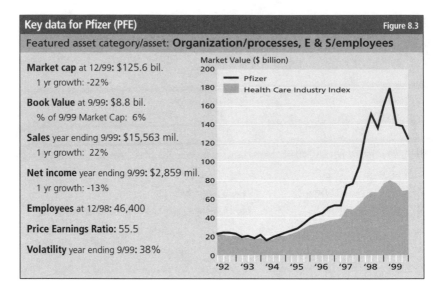

Key data for Pfizer (PFE)   Figure 8.3

Featured asset category/asset: **Organization/processes, E & S/employees**

Market cap at 12/99: $125.6 bil.

1 yr growth: -22%

Book Value at 9/99: $8.8 bil.

% of 9/99 Market Cap: 6%

Sales year ending 9/99: $15,563 mil.

1 yr growth: 22%

Net income year ending 9/99: $2,859 mil.

1 yr growth: -13%

Employees at 12/98: 46,400

Price Earnings Ratio: 55.5

Volatility year ending 9/99: 38%

ment—among them, drugs for the treatment of cancer, depression, diabetes, obesity, and stroke.[8]

On average, it takes pharmaceutical companies 190 person-years to move a compound through the various stages from discovery to clinical trials. In the industry overall, just one out of every 7 million compounds that undergo screening actually gets to the shelves of drugstores.

At Pfizer, the process takes less than a third of the average time. And in its determination to keep its product pipeline full, the company is constantly elaborating and improving upon the intense, focused series of actions that push ideas toward their ultimate fate as products or also-rans.

With dozens of compounds going through the Pfizer testing process at any one time, one major challenge is to discard, as early in the process as possible, those that aren't going to make the grade. But researchers who have spent years bringing a compound along often have an emotional commitment to an idea and a project, and they battle to keep it alive.

Pfizer has devised a way to cope with this problem, thereby making the most of its drug-testing process and paving the way to increased value. A so-called step chart is set up for each potential drug, indicating the number of encouraging compounds that should be in hand at every stage. The charts help everyone involved in a project see how it is doing and what still needs to be done. They also serve as exhibit A when managers target a faltering project for extinction, and the project's scientists protest.

The payoff for this increased vigilance? A stable full of strong-selling

drugs, which has given Pfizer confidence. The company forecasts compound annual growth of 16 percent in revenues and 20 percent in income
from 1999 to 2002—the highest of the 10 largest pharmaceutical companies. (See Figure 8.3.)

Similar process skills are needed by venture-capital firms that screen
hundreds of business plans to find the ones in which they will invest. Like
pharmaceutical companies, they, too, have to know when it's time to kill
off projects in which they have invested time, money, and emotion.

Ⓠ How do we define a system?

Systems are a necessary fact of human life. We have a circulatory
system, a digestive system, a respiratory system, and others. Each
requires input in order to produce output. Without them, our bodies
would collapse.

And so it is with business systems. An information system might be
likened to the body's central nervous system, for example, transmitting
messages and important pieces of information throughout the enterprise. Business systems embody the operational rules that keep an organization's parts running smoothly and efficiently. The enormity of the
task becomes clear when one considers that those parts include interre-
lated, interacting, or interdependent mechanical, electrical, electronic,
and logical components.

Since the advent of the computer, the operational rules have come to
be embedded in technology. But when we speak of systems, we don't
mean hardware. Rather, we are referring to the codified knowledge that
assembles, organizes, and directs the flow of information.

Q: Who is creating value with systems?
A: The Procter & Gamble Company.

As the 1990s got under way, The Procter & Gamble Company, based
in Cincinnati, Ohio, was a global giant of awesome proportions. The
world's largest maker of household products, P&G could point to operations in more than 40 countries in Europe, Asia, Africa, and Latin America. As a matter of fact, 1991 marked a milestone of sorts for the com-

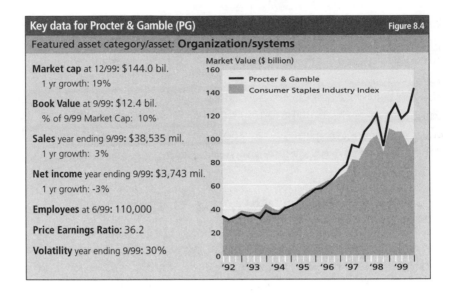

Key data for Procter & Gamble (PG)   Figure 8.4

Featured asset category/asset: **Organization/systems**

Market Value ($ billion)

Market cap at 12/99: $144.0 bil.
  1 yr growth: 19%

Book Value at 9/99: $12.4 bil.
  % of 9/99 Market Cap: 10%

Sales year ending 9/99: $38,535 mil.
  1 yr growth: 3%

Net income year ending 9/99: $3,743 mil.
  1 yr growth: -3%

Employees at 6/99: 110,000

Price Earnings Ratio: 36.2

Volatility year ending 9/99: 30%

— Procter & Gamble
▮ Consumer Staples Industry Index

'92 '93 '94 '95 '96 '97 '98 '99

pany. That is when sales from outside the United States first contributed more than half of the company's total revenues.

But as this corporate Godzilla soon discovered, more is not always better, particularly when the infrastructure isn't up to the task of managing distribution channels. Domestically, P&G had long profited from a system that allowed for direct sales to giant retailers like Wal-Mart Stores, Inc. But that was not the case in certain of its big overseas markets.

In Asia, for instance, hundreds of third-party distributors handled a majority of the company's sales. Many were small family businesses that processed orders, handled billing, and managed inventory. In Central and Eastern Europe, too, P&G depended on thousands of wholesalers to distribute its products.

The situation was so chaotic that, in 1992, P&G managers in these regions independently concluded that they could not meet their corporate mandate for growth unless some changes were made. Each decided to switch over to a smaller number of exclusive P&G distributors, which they would help to become more efficient, computerized businesses.

Out of these efforts grew a major initiative to improve organization effectiveness and keep P&G's products competitive in the global arena. By using an asset it calls Distributor Business Systems (DBS) for ordering, shipping, and inventory management, the company has transformed a cumbersome third-party system into a value-creating advantage.

Seeking to expand P&G's reach, ensure a loyal distribution network, and provide sales data vital to the business, P&G's managers selected an ordering, shipping, and billing package that runs on personal computers. The package also supports a continuous replenishment system similar to that which the company uses in the United States.

The new-value payoff has been enormous.

On investments in Asia and Central and Eastern Europe, P&G realized a net profit in excess of $100 million.

With accurate pricing and product specifications that are automatically updated every day, haphazard distributor replenishment is a thing of the past. As for P&G's performance, the company now markets 300 brands in more than 140 countries, with on-the-ground operations in 70 countries. The company generated $38.5 billion in revenues in the year ending third quarter of 1999, and net income of $3.7 billion. Investors applauded this showing by paying 36 times earnings and nearly 10 times book value to buy a share of P&G, generating a market capitalization of $144 billion at year-end 1999.[9] (See Figure 8.4.)

Ⓠ How do we define culture and values?

"My primary challenge during these years," Lawrence A. Bossidy, former chairman and chief executive officer of AlliedSignal, Inc. and now chairman of Honeywell International, once told an audience, "has been the same as the one that no doubt faces many companies . . . that is to say, creating a culture in which people focus on where they are going, instead of where they have been."

Instilling the "right stuff" isn't easy.

Both culture and values are key organization assets. We define values as an organization's guiding principles or minimum negotiable standards of behavior. They help employees to make sound decisions without the need for constant cross-checking and bureaucracy. And they hold the potential for rewarding companies with new sources of value.

Witness our case in point.

Q: Who is creating value with culture and values?

A: Johnson & Johnson.

What holds Johnson & Johnson's decentralized businesses together is its 308-word code of ethics called "our credo." A copy of it is literally carved in stone at the company's New Brunswick headquarters. The credo tells everyone in the organization which people and which principles to care about—in that order.

"We believe our first responsibility is to the doctors, nurses, and patients, and to the mothers and fathers," it begins. Johnson & Johnson employees and the communities in which the company operates occupy the second and third places. Stockholders come last, after suppliers and distributors, but that's not really an insult. The credo declares that shareholders will get a fair return if those other constituents get first priority.

An increase of 30 percent in market capitalization since mid-1998 suggests that the credo, and the culture built around it, are effective assets for creating value at Johnson & Johnson. The company's belief in managing its businesses for the long-term enables its managers to function with less fear of making mistakes.

⬤ How do we define a brand?

These days, Robert W. Pittman, president and chief operating officer of America Online, Inc., likes to say, "brands win." And he speaks from experience. In a 1997 survey of Americans, 41 percent of respondents identified the America Online name without any prompting. And the AOL brand dwarfed those of its competitors, including Microsoft Corporation's Microsoft Network. AOL subscribers on average spend an hour a day on-line.

Brands are an essential source of value for companies. They are often thought of as what we call "customer assets" and defined as the intangible sum of a product's attributes based on the way it is sold or advertised in the marketplace (its name, packaging, price, image, and so forth). But we think brands should be defined more broadly in the New Economy—that is, as your reputation, as the result of the interactions of your employees with customers and suppliers, as the external manifestation of your strategy and culture.

Brands need to be managed on an organization-wide basis. They are as much the responsibility of the chief executive officer as the head of marketing. We include brands as an organization asset because they relate as much to a company's ideas, culture, employees, and suppliers as to its customers.[10]

Q: **Who is creating value with brands?**

A: **Starbucks Corporation.**

What makes the Starbucks story so powerful is this: It transformed a common cup of coffee into one of the most valuable brands in the world.

"The equity of the Starbucks brand," says Howard Schultz, who acquired Starbucks in 1987, "is a priceless asset." Oddly enough, Schultz never set out to build a brand. His goal was to build a company.

"Then one day I started getting calls. 'Can you come and tell us how you built a national brand in only five years?' It was unusual, people told me, for a brand to burst onto the national consciousness as quickly as Starbucks had. When I looked back, I realized we had fashioned a brand in a way no business-school textbook could ever have prescribed."

He spent little on advertising—not because he didn't believe in it, but because he couldn't afford it. "Instead," Schultz says, "we concentrated on creating value and customer service....Our success proves you

"... Our success proves you can build a national brand without 30-second sound-bites"

can build a national brand without 30-second sound bites. . . . It proves that the best way to build a brand is one customer at a time."

Today the $1.7-billion-a-year chain maximizes its brand beyond its stores. "Our goal," explains Schultz, "is to make our coffee available where people shop, travel, play, and work."

Starbucks products are offered through a mail-order catalog and on-line via America Online and the World Wide Web. The company sells Starbucks beans to grocery stores, restaurants, airlines, and hotels. The brand line has been extended with the addition of Starbucks Frappuccino, a bottled coffee drink, and a premium ice cream (coffee-flavored, of course).

The distinctive Starbucks logo can be found on everything from storefronts to the cup of coffee a passenger is served on an airplane. And the brand image doesn't stop with the logo. Every store has a comfortable décor, a warm color scheme, and inviting aromas that beg customers to linger. That aura of good feelings is a carefully designed part of the brand, too.

It is no surprise that Starbucks has reaped enormous value from its brand. "Three months after we introduced our Starbucks gourmet ice cream nationally," says Schultz, "we became the number one premium [coffee-flavored] ice cream in the country."

Ice cream lovers aren't the only ones enjoying a Starbucks premium. The company, whose annual revenues rose 28 percent to $1.7 billion through the third quarter of 1999, generated net income of $102 million, an increase of 49 percent.

Ⓠ How do we define proprietary knowledge?

"Everything that can be invented," Charles H. Duell, commissioner of the U.S. Office of Patents, once boldly proclaimed, "has been invented."

The year was 1899. And Duell was urging William McKinley, then president of the United States, to abolish the patent office. Fortunately, McKinley resisted the idea. So has every subsequent U.S. president. Never in history has a company's proprietary knowledge been more essential and more vulnerable than it is today.

How do we define proprietary knowledge? Simply this way: It is any concept, idea, invention, literary creation, software program, or other artistic or creative work that is definable, measurable, and exclusive in nature.

Companies by the dozens around the world are making the most of these assets, creating new value for their businesses. Among them: Xerox Corporation.

"Building and sharing knowledge," says Paul A. Allaire, its chairman and then-chief executive officer, "may well be the most important source of competitive advantage as we approach the dawn of the 21st century." [11]

He speaks from experience. Xerox received some 1,046 patents in 1998, or more than three a day. Here is another example.

Q: Who is creating value with proprietary knowledge?
A: Idealab!

One company devoted solely to the business of proprietary knowledge is idealab!, a company we introduced in Chapter 2. When founder Bill Gross rhapsodizes about "playing" with ideas all day long, it is easy to forget that there is still a reality-based, hard-edged business side to his venture. And considering that his playground happens to be the fast-paced, no-holds-barred Internet, the edges can be hard indeed.

Recognizing the precarious nature of the virtual life, idealab!'s proprietary-knowledge mantra can be summed up in one word—speed. Appraise ideas fast and develop the good ones into Internet-related companies even faster. To that end, Gross has assembled a group of brainy advisers to help sift through the multitude of ideas that spill from his head.

Once an idea has been given the green light, Gross leverages his proprietary knowledge by making sure that the budding entrepreneurs he chooses to head his ventures focus their valuable time and energy on developing their core businesses.

Everything else, from protecting intellectual property to lining up office space is included in the package of support services—what Gross calls "Internet start-up in a box"—that idealab! provides to every new enterprise.

Gross's novel approach to the mundane details involved in getting a company up and running allows the various CEOs to hit the ground creating from day one. As the head of one idealab! start-up told *Inc.* magazine, "If I hadn't been with idealab!, I would have put in a lot more time working with lawyers, working on names and trademarks, working on incorporation papers, working on a logo." Instead, only a few weeks after first talking with Bill Gross, this executive was busy creating a prototype of a needed Web interface.

Bill Gross has been creating value with proprietary knowledge since he was a teenager—the 40-something entrepreneur paid for college by selling patented stereo speakers he designed himself. Perhaps that's why he so intimately understands that freeing up creators to create is the best way to turn ideas into proprietary knowledge that can pay big dividends in the marketplace.

▶ What's next?

Having explored how each of the five asset categories contributes to a company's portfolio, we now expand our focus.

While reading these success stories, you might have wondered: What questions should my company ask? What actions should we take to increase the value of our organization in the New Economy?

In Part III, we help you put it all together. Remember, you don't invest in assets in isolation. When it comes to business models, the whole should be greater than the sum of the parts. The mix and interaction of the assets in which a company invests—both tangible and intangible—are among the most critical drivers of value creation.

As we steer you through the steps of managing what matters to create value, we remind you of the four realities of the New Economy:

- New business models are emerging, based on unique combinations of assets, including technologies. Businesses are their assets—all of their assets, tangible and intangible.

- New business models create new risks. But risk in the New Economy encompasses upside opportunity as well as downside threat.

- New processes and tools are needed to manage both new business models and new risks. How a company builds and manages its unique portfolio of assets is what drives economic success.

- Transparency of information is vital to value creation in the New Economy. But decision makers need better access to information than what they are getting today.

In the chapters ahead, we consider the actions you need to take to respond to these new realities. We examine the four principal challenges you face if you are to maximize your value creation.

Ask Yourself:

- Consider your company's organization assets. Are you effectively managing these assets to create value?

- How does your company's mix of organization assets work within its business model to create value?

- Do the case studies in this chapter suggest ways that your company might manage its organization assets more effectively?

- How does your company track and measure the value-creating contribution of its organization assets?

- What are best practices in your industry when it comes to managing organization assets? How do your competitors gain advantage with organization assets?

❑

Manage What Matters

9

Putting it All Together.

"If you want
to do something
new, you have
to stop doing
something old."

—Peter Drucker

W hen Daniel C. Ferguson took the helm at the Newell Company back in 1965, the Freeport, Illinois-based manufacturer made curtain rods and not much else. It sold around $14 million worth of product, mostly to old-time retailers like Woolworth and Kresge.

Ferguson had something more in mind. Aware of the trend toward ever-bigger retail chains, and eager to expand the company's product line, Ferguson set Newell on the path that would eventually carry it into the ranks of the Fortune 500.

Specifically, Ferguson saw that Newell excelled at producing low-cost, high-volume products and selling them to large retailers. More importantly, he recognized that he could add value to the organization by leveraging Newell's particular strengths through a series of acquisitions.

"A combination or package of lines going to the large retailers carries more marketing impact than each line separately," Ferguson declared. So he set out to ramp up Newell's growth by investing in a portfolio of tangible and intangible assets that would fulfill his strategic vision.

Over the past three decades, the company has acquired more than 75 companies (18 major acquisitions in the 1990s alone), including a deal in March 1999 that brought Rubbermaid into the fold. As the company (rechristened Newell Rubbermaid, Inc.) takes each newcomer under its wing, it imparts its particular take on manufacturing and sales processes—what it calls "Newellization"—to bring the acquiree up to Newell standards of profitability. The result: on average, newcomers' operating margins triple, from 5 percent to 15 percent.[1]

And Newell's sales and earnings just grow and grow. Over the years, annual sales climbed from $14 million to $5.8 billion through the third quarter-1999. Meanwhile, the company's market capitalization was $8.2 billion at year-end 1999.

Newell now turns out dozens of disparate branded products, from hair barrettes to venetian blinds to cookware to office products. The product list might seem to make Newell a confusing chorus of voices,

> ## Newell thrives in the New Economy because it combines its process assets, customer assets, and brand assets into a potent, value-creating brew.

but no matter. The products themselves are not what caught our eye. Rather, it is the way the company continuously reinvents its portfolio of assets to maximize value.

For example, when one of its more profitable purchases, Wm. E. Wright, Inc., a West Warren, Massachusetts, maker of home-sewing products, began selling largely to specialty shops, Newell got rid of it. The company no longer fit into its core strategy of selling large-volume products to major retailers.

Ninety-eight-year-old Newell continues to thrive in the New Economy because it combines its process assets (Newellization) with its customer assets (big discount chains like Wal-Mart), and its brand assets (Mirro, Goody, Little Tikes, and Levolor, to name but a few) into a potent, value-creating brew.

Clearly, Newell lives by the premise we introduced in Part I of the book—companies are their assets, all of them, both tangible and intangible. The company also recognizes one of the prime principles of value creation we presented in Part II—the necessity to constantly fine-tune its economic DNA to make sure it has the right mix of assets in a changing and ever-increasingly volatile marketplace.

That is why a number of the companies we featured in Part II showed up in more than one case study. The ultimate success of companies like Dell, Amazon, Schwab, and Starbucks depends not on their ability to make the most of one or two assets, but on their skill in optimizing all assets that make up their business models, including relationships with employees, suppliers, investors and customers.

Now, in Part III, we address a challenge every company must face: creating a business model for the New Economy.

That is the essential achievement of many of the winners of the 1990s that has led to the emergence of upstart supernovas like Cisco and AOL. It is no accident that their stock prices soared 124,825 percent and 81,400 percent respectively over the course of that decade. They produced unprecedented value for their investors through highly inventive, business models that others now try to imitate.

In times past, companies often looked at change as incremental, asking "how do we improve what we are already doing?" Each new wave of management innovations became part of the organizational canon. A process view of business introduced by reengineering, for example, added to the insights of Total Quality Management (TQM). Best practices helped to codify processes and capabilities. These innovations helped companies with improving "how" they performed—but not necessarily with determining "what" to do.

Therein lies the challenge in the New Economy.

Companies need to know "what" courses to take during a time of fundamental economic change. Nothing short of a new business model will be sufficient to succeed.

The problem is, business management is too often handicapped by misperceptions as to the basic elements of the organization, the appropriate relationships among those elements, and the organization's connection to its market in terms of what creates and destroys value. Let's take a look at each in turn.

! An Incomplete View of the Enterprise.

Few managers fully understand that companies are built from essential building blocks of assets, the processes used, and the measurement systems that record success. It's important to see how assets relate to processes, how processes connect to outcomes, and how measurements relate to market results. Otherwise, companies can become unrelated collections of assets and processes. They lose track of their own basic building blocks, their company's economic DNA.

! An Incomplete View of Strategy.

With an eye focused primarily on product and market strategy, business leaders have overlooked views encompassing other assets. Moreover, changes in the economic and social environment have fundamentally altered the intrinsic business value of different assets—both tangible and intangible.

! An Incomplete Understanding of the Market.

Companies are often not linked—or are only loosely connected—to their market environment. Even sophisticated enterprise resource planning software does not integrate relevant market data or industry best practices. Management lacks the ability to link internal and external data and insights—on all key assets, processes and outcomes, let alone in real-time.

! An Incomplete View of Value.

Companies do not have a comprehensive view of what creates or destroys value. Nor can management typically identify all the sources of value to the company, both internally and externally. The result: Leadership has an incomplete view of how to achieve market rewards.

How do companies resolve these four "disconnects?" Our solution is an asset-based view of strategy. We believe every organization needs to create a business model that links combinations of assets to value creation.

Using the lens of Value Dynamics, you can gain insight into strategy development by simply looking at events in the marketplace from the view of assets. Why did AOL propose a merger with Time Warner? To acquire more customers by linking new sets of assets, including content offerings supported by broadband capabilities. Why does the frenzy of IPOs continue? Because investors increasingly understand the risk and return of these new investment opportunities. Why are companies outsourcing today? To gain new efficiencies in the value chain, which free them to focus on development of their core assets. Why are companies offering stock options to employees? To acquire and retain employee assets and their knowledge in a world at war over talent.

Of course every company is unique. But some truths are universal. Every company must learn to make the most of the full range of its assets, not expecting to simply migrate from left to right, from tangible

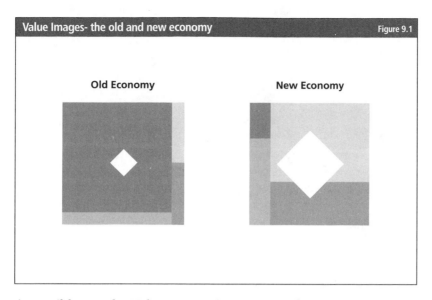

Value Images- the old and new economy Figure 9.1

Old Economy   New Economy

to intangible, on the Value Dynamics map. And every company must recognize that how it weights its portfolio with different combinations of assets will decide its economic outcome. Once a company understands how the elements in that portfolio come together and interact to create value, it can set about redesigning its business genome.

To help you see the whole picture, we have developed a visual technique called Value Imaging. It provides a new and graphic way of envisioning business models past, present, and future.

In an industrial economy, for example, a typical business might make heavy investments in physical, capital-intensive assets. In contrast, a business in the New Economy (dot.coms) is more likely to emphasize investments in intangibles like intellectual property, brands, systems, and relationships, as depicted in Figure 9.1 above.

Some companies that have historically been classified in different industries—say, Amazon and Dell—may be quite similar in terms of what assets they use to create value. Value Imaging shows that conceptually. Consider the representation of the business models of Amazon, Borders and Dell in Figure 9.2 on the next page.

The figures we use for the value contributed by the different asset categories are, of course, only estimates. No organization is currently providing exact data of this nature. Nor is that data broadly available. Still, some important inferences can be drawn.

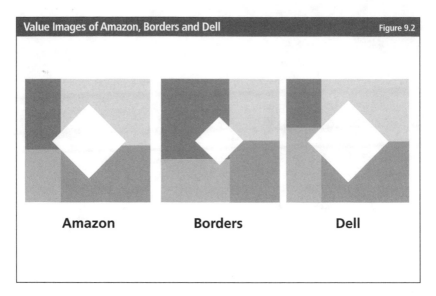

Value Images of Amazon, Borders and Dell   Figure 9.2

Amazon   Borders   Dell

The three companies above show substantial differences in the value contributed by physical assets. Dell relies on them the least. Amazon, which you might think relies solely on virtual assets, has begun investing increasing sums in physical assets, principally state-of-the-art warehouses to promote speedy distribution. The value proposition of Borders continues to depend on its large chain of bookstores, even with its announcements about adding digital media. Hence its heavy investments in physical assets.

Using this graphic depiction, Value Imaging shows conceptually the estimated value contributed by the five asset categories. But this technique can also be used to depict many other inputs and outputs, examples of which include the monetary investment in assets, management time expended on them, or degree of risk for each asset category in a business model.

As we journey through the steps involved in managing what matters, Part III explores the challenges involved in responding to the realities of the New Economy. Put another way, your organization needs to have a coherent, integrated approach to the four challenges of value creation in this new century:

→ Design your business model for value creation.
→ Master risk in an uncertain environment.
→ Manage your business as a portfolio of assets.
→ Use information, measure and report all your assets.

These four challenges (our shorthand for them is strategy, risk, processes, and information) do not exist in splendid isolation. As Figure 9.3 illustrates, each is logically linked to the other three, and all work in concert. In fact, we urge you to view Figure 9.3 three-dimensionally, rather than in two dimensions, to fully understand the dynamic relationship of these four challenges.

Companies need to align strategy, risk management, processes, and information for decision-making. Your business model will be robust only if all of these activities are in balance.

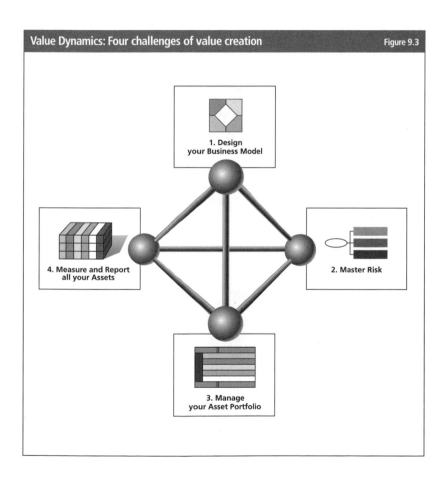

Value Dynamics: Four challenges of value creation — Figure 9.3

1. Design your Business Model

4. Measure and Report all your Assets

2. Master Risk

3. Manage your Asset Portfolio

▶ What's next?

In the following chapter, we suggest how you can design and build a business model for value creation in the New Economy.

Imagine for a moment what your business model of the future might look like. Put on your strategy hat and ask yourself what combination of physical, financial, employee and supplier, and customer assets you want and need to create new value. Then think about which technologies and organization assets should be used to connect, leverage, and enable this portfolio.

Now, turn the page.

Ask Yourself:

- Does your company integrate strategy, risk management, processes and information in a single model or view?

- Does your company's planning process address all of its assets and the way they interact to create value?

- What does your company's business model look like today in terms of value contributed by the five asset categories (financial, physical, employee & supplier, customer and organization)?

- What are your competitors' weaknesses and how might your future business model exploit them?

10

Design Your
Business Model.

"Things
should be
made as simple
as possible,
but not any
simpler."
—Albert Einstein

I n the summer of 1999, a much-publicized battle to acquire U. S. West, one of the last independent Baby Bells, was won by Qwest Communications International, Inc., an upstart fiber-optics communications company based in Denver, Colorado.

The stakes were high as players across the industry jockeyed to become broadband mega-carriers in the twenty-first century.

Joseph Nacchio, former president of AT&T Corporation and current chairman and chief executive officer of Qwest, explained in an interview that his company's pursuit of U. S. West was "not a question of cash flows and growth. It's a question of putting the right combination of assets together. . . ." [1]

What assets did Qwest gain when it acquired U. S. West, the carrier that serves customers in 14 Western and Midwestern states? Certainly, Qwest provided the final broadband "mile" in U. S. West's campaign to bring Internet-based communications into homes and businesses across the United States. But U.S. West had also purchased a large and growing customer base.

With the acquisition, and the assets that accompanied it, Qwest effectively redesigned its business model. The key point, as Qwest's management understands, is that some business models create more value than others—and the winners today are those building powerful new combinations of assets to create value for their entire value chain, including customers, employees, and investors.

In fact, many leading companies are intuitively meeting the first challenge of succeeding in the New Economy: Design your business model for value creation.

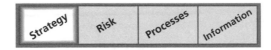

Value Dynamics helps organizations to integrate diverse approaches and methodologies within a common, asset-based perspective on value creation. That kind of integration is invaluable at a time when traditional industry and geographic boundaries are dissolving, turning the rules of business upside down. It will go a long way to helping management overcome uncertainty to see clear courses of action.

This view is distinct from the traditional view of strategy as involving a bottom-line view of products/markets, effectiveness or efficiency of processes, and top-line growth. We suggest that strategy should be asset-centric and value-centric. Companies succeed to varying degrees

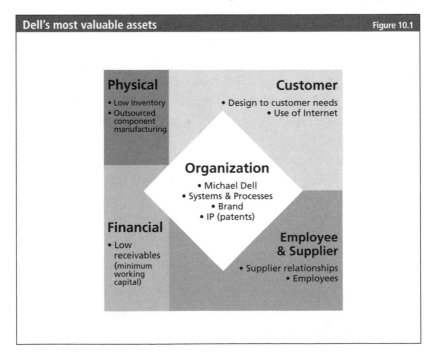

Dell's most valuable assets   Figure 10.1

Physical
• Low inventory
• Outsourced component manufacturing

Customer
• Design to customer needs
• Use of Internet

Organization
• Michael Dell
• Systems & Processes
• Brand
• IP (patents)

Financial
• Low receivables (minimum working capital)

Employee & Supplier
• Supplier relationships
• Employees

based on extracting value from investments in all five asset classes. Consider Dell, for example. Figure 10.1 is a hypothetical Value Image showing the estimated value contributed in each of the asset classes. Dell's "Be Direct" business model derives its value from the interconnectedness of all its asset strategies:

- **Customer Assets.** Significant value is derived from Dell's strategy of custom designing each computer and delivering it direct to the customer, together with Dell's leading-edge use of the Internet to connect its customers and suppliers.

- **Employee and Supplier Assets.** Dell's strategy of outsourcing much of its operations requires it to build strong supplier relationships in virtually all aspects of the business.

- **Physical Assets.** Dell's customer and supply chain strategies allow it to minimize costs tied up in inventory.

- **Financial Assets.** A relatively small investment in financial assets reflects the impact of Dell's supply-chain and customer strategies on its capital requirements and working capital.

- **Organization Assets.** Dell's system and process assets effectively support its business plan. These assets include a cornerstone of the company's success: Michael Dell's leadership. Dell has also sought dozens of patents for its business model, including the on-line ordering system and methods used in "contiguous flow" operations.

Historically, companies in particular industries have tended to invest in and extract value from certain types of assets. Companies in the same industry, as a result, have had similar asset portfolios and similar results. Those patterns are changing, however.

During the 1990s, for example, many banks and other financial services organizations divested themselves of physical assets in favor of electronic banking and information services. Mainstream manufacturers outsourced manufacturing operations to focus on their intangible assets, such as brands and intellectual property. Professional services firms, which were leveraging employee time and knowledge, began to deploy financial assets to build venture capital funds. And Internet e-tailers, as we've noted, were making big investments in physical assets to gain better distribution.

Business Models Break The Rules:

Adventurous companies have defied one of the most important mantras of business: Never sell your products or services for less than what they cost to produce and deliver. They are giving them away to acquire other important assets, including customers.

Example: Around 1900, King Gillette, a traveling salesman, broke new ground when he invented the safety razor and the disposable razor blade. The eponymous company he formed first packaged the razor and blades together. Then Gillette's leaders made a key decision: They gave away millions of razors, thereby triggering a demand that has remained strong to this day.

Example: After Marc Andreessen teamed up with Jim Clark to form Netscape Communications Corporation in 1994, the two men decided to let users download the Netscape Navigator browser for a free 90-day trial, rather than sell the software for $99. They never looked back. Netscape quickly established itself as a leader in the on-line market, revolutionizing access to the Internet. By March 1998, some 100 million copies of Netscape Navigator had been downloaded, most at no cost.[2]

Example: Free-PC, Inc. (an idealab! company) emulated Gillette's strategy a century later when it announced that it would give free personal computers to 10,000 people. The only "cost" was intangible: Users would have to supply a detailed information profile about themselves and be willing to allow a small portion of the screen to be used for advertisements tailored to their expressed interests. Half a million people visited the company's Web site within the first two days of the offer. For Free-PC, the primary asset is the audience of users who view ads.[3]

Example: In October 1999, Encyclopedia Britannica decided to give away the contents of its 32-volume reference set, which retailed in book form for $1,300. Britannica.com, Inc., the spin-off running the Internet site, anticipates advertising revenues of $35 million per year. During the site's first week of operation, log-on attempts totaled 10 million a day.[4]

As noted earlier, our research—combined with abundant market evidence—shows that intangible assets have become increasingly important during the past 20 years, while tangible assets have contributed proportionally less in terms of value creation and more in terms of risk. In short, the risk-and-reward ratio of different assets is changing rapidly.

In this chapter, our mission is to outline the key steps in designing your business model for the New Economy. Remember, you need to see your enterprise as a portfolio of assets that extends well beyond the boundaries of your organization, to include the entire value chain of relationships. In the process, you will need to consider three questions:

➜ **What assets are you using and what value do they contribute?**

➜ **What assets do you need to succeed in the New Economy?**

➜ **What asset portfolio strategies should you use to succeed?**

Remember what Peter Lynch admonished investors: "Know what you own, and why you own it." That's a good place to begin this journey.

ⓠ What assets are you using?

Begin by examining your organization's most important sources of value. Your challenge is to inventory the 25 assets defined in the Value Dynamics Framework, as well as others of importance to your business. In doing so, you are clearing a path for an asset-centric strategic planning exercise using the five asset classes as a lens. This first step should produce insight into your assets on four key dimensions:

- What are your historical investments in these assets?
- Where do the assets reside in your company?
- How are they currently managed?
- What is the value they have contributed?

An examination of your company's expenditures is a good place to begin. How your company spends money is a key indicator of what it values. Determine the proportional financial investments that are made in various assets—but remember that your company's investment also includes time.

To start, examine the assets listed (at book value) on the balance sheet. But take note: The job may be more complicated than you think. Although book assets appear relatively easy to assess from your accounting records, those that contribute the most to value may not have the highest book value or be the most expensive.

Securing detailed information about assets not on the balance sheet, including your investments in intangible assets, will probably require considerably more investigation. You will need sources of information that are not fed by the company's traditional information and management systems.

To estimate the value contributed by customer assets, you can look to several sources. They include revenue produced and measures of profitability by customer, which may be readily available through current revenue reporting and cost accounting. You will need to track the

> **Securing detailed information about assets not on the balance sheet will probably require considerably more investigation.**

amount you spend on various sales and marketing activities. If your company has invested in a customer relationship management system, you have a head start. But remember, much of the value derived from managing or investing in your customer relationships may not be classified as sales and marketing costs.

Similarly, you should be able to identify the amount you spend on your employee and supplier assets by looking at activities such as hiring and training of employees and managing the entire supply chain. If your company has an integrated supply chain management system, you may have some idea about the value contributed by suppliers. (Again, note that your current expenditures are not necessarily a good guide to your long-term investments in these assets. For example, you may spend substantial sums to acquire a supplier or employee, who will bring benefits for many years, so your investment may generate economic returns over the life of the relationship.)

In the case of organization assets, your approximations are less likely to be dollar-specific. You may be able to identify your expenditure on processes and systems, but you are unlikely to be able to isolate the dollars expended on sustaining your culture and values. (We doubt you have information systems for these assets.) This means you will be more dependent on informed estimates about the importance of each asset in the organization asset category.

Even on difficult-to-measure intangible assets, management needs to have an opinion on the value they contribute.

Benchmarking data from companies with similar business models and strategies often helps managers understand their own investment in and management of their important assets. Such data, which includes best practices information, provides important comparative information pointing to "how your organization is doing" against the best in the marketplace. In turn, this information supports the next stage in designing a business model.

🅠 What assets do you need to succeed?

The challenge of defining an overall strategy—and translating it into a vision, goals, and actions for the company—begins with fundamental questions about your company's current business model, and whether you can increase its value in five strategic areas:

- Expanding into new product or service markets.
- Leveraging your own resources alone or in combination with those of other companies.
- Changing or expanding the types of products you market, including moving from physical products to intellectual products.
- Adding new technologies and processes to connect and scale your assets to achieve the best value-creating synergies.
- Expanding access to assets by using partners and additional channels.

To succeed, your company will need to understand the strategic preferences implied by investing in certain types of assets and ignoring others—and the practical consequences of those investment decisions. You will also need to weigh the risks, keeping in mind that failure to act may be the most risky business of all.

In a dynamic environment, every strategy that maintains the *status quo* may be under threat. Competitors—seen and unseen—even now are developing ways to acquire some of your most valuable assets, including your workforce talent and customers. No business model can be regarded as "safe," because the most important assets today are people, whose value generally increases as relationships become more enduring. Customers, employees, suppliers and investors will migrate to the companies that create the most value for them.

When developing your strategy for the New Economy, take note of both your old and new competitors. While the market is focused on the dizzying growth of dot.coms and other emerging enterprises, the real revolution may come as Industrial Age giants respond to new opportunities. Sweeping change is inevitable as large and long-established companies, with their enormous untapped asset bases, wake up to the realities of today's economy and begin to do smart asset management.

In an article in *The Wall Street Journal*, Lou Gerstner, chairman and chief executive officer of IBM, described the new dot.com companies as "fireflies before the storm—all stirred up, throwing off sparks."

He continued: "The real story that's arriving—the real disturbance in the force—is when the thousands and thousands of institutions that exist today seize the power of this global computing and communications infrastructure and use it to transform themselves. That's the real revolution."[5]

Gerstner went on to tell the analysts about a visit to IBM's headquarters by the entire management team of Royal Philips Electronics, the Netherlands-based conglomerate. The purpose? To discuss how to turn Philips into an eBusiness that leverages all its assets, including customers, brands, suppliers, and patents.

Q What asset portfolio strategies should you deploy?

The third step points to the tactics, which will help you implement your business model for success. We distinguish here between the overall strategy that guides the design of your business model, on the one hand, and portfolio strategies for implementing a business model.

There are countless portfolio asset strategies that companies can use to create or enhance the value of assets that comprise the business model. To start you thinking about asset strategies, however, we have identified five basic strategies you can apply to individual or multiple assets.

All management strategies, we hold, are fundamentally asset-portfolio strategies, even though they are seldom seen in that light. These strategies are designed to highlight and improve the value of specific assets as they interact and enhance the value of your business as a whole.

In a merger or acquisition, for example, a company acquires an entire asset portfolio, presumably for less money or in less time than it would take to build the portfolio itself. It is a make-or-buy decision. By identifying specific asset-based strategies, we hope to help you see the range of strategic planning possibilities.

The first of these portfolio strategies entails *building* assets by developing or creating new sources of value. The second strategy involves *enhancing* assets—for example, by using a new performance management system to improve employee efficiency and productivity. Using the third strategy, you *connect* an asset to other assets—for instance, by allowing your customers to place orders directly with suppliers. Next, you can *convert* an asset to a different function—by using customers as salespeople, for example, or by reconfiguring an idle plant to turn out a new product. Finally, you can adopt a *blocking* strategy, which means that you exploit an asset to make it more costly and complicated for a company to build an asset portfolio that can successfully compete against yours.

Each of these portfolio strategies can be applied to all of the assets in the five asset categories. For purposes of illustration, however, we have chosen an example for each strategy to show what one company has done.

As you read these case studies, imagine how these portfolio strategies could be applied to other assets—or to your own organization.

We start with an organization that has become a New Economy success story when it comes to building assets, CMGI, Inc. This high-profile company incubates Internet IPOs, both in the business-to-consumer and business-to-business arenas.

Strategy: Build

A company can build assets in diverse ways. Consider the potential of adding new competencies to formulate a new research and development process. In turn, the R&D team creates a new knowledge base for the company that contributes to a larger reservoir of intellectual assets, which may be in turn codified in the form of patents, or products and services for licensing. IBM, as a result of an intensive intellectual property effort, earns almost $1 billion, or over 10 percent of its annual pretax profits, from licensing its intellectual property. Those funds are primarily free cash flow, generating a recurring net revenue stream.[6]

On the other hand, a dot.com company might build an asset base almost out of thin air by networking unrelated companies and building a customer base atop that foundation. In fact, that was the route taken by CMGI, Inc., an early backer of Internet portals.

CMGI's strategy centers on identifying what chief executive officer David S. Wetherell calls "viral Web sites," meaning sites at which information (and thus value) grows simply through use and replication.[7] In other words, Internet users visit sites and provide information, which expands the asset base.

CMGI has been able to build this viral empire because Wetherell understood how to turn undervalued Internet upstarts into a value-creating asset

> **CMGI has been able to build this viral empire because Wetherell understood how to turn Internet upstarts into a value-creating asset base.**

base. In 1996, for example, he saw the potential of Lycos, Inc., investing $2 million in the Web gateway. That investment has since produced $6 billion in Lycos shares, some of which were held by CMGI and others traded.

Wetherell was also among the first to recognize the value of GeoCities, in which CMGI invested $4.1 million in cash in 1995. Four years later, when GeoCities was sold to Yahoo!, it was valued at $1 billion.

Other CMGI acquisitions include a 30 percent stake in Ancestry.com, Inc., a Utah-based genealogy-research firm, purchased for just $10 million. Ancestry's MyFamily.com Web site provides a vehicle for extended families to share information, which puts it squarely in Wetherell's camp because it generates value simply through use by growing numbers of people.

CMGI is a diversified network of Internet companies that share market information, technologies, skills, and other resources, and also do business with one another. Its build strategy has, in effect, turned it into an "equity incubator." CMGI nurtures Internet companies, in expectation of an IPO or a sale.

The company today represents the most diverse network of Internet enterprises. Since 1995, it has funded more than 60 synergistic companies through its venture capital affiliate. In addition, it owns or has a majority control in 16 operating companies.

CMGI's market capitalization at mid-1997 was $158 million. By the beginning of the year 2000, it had climbed to $34 billion.

Strategy: Enhance

Industrial psychologists have spent their lives seeking ways to quantify the experience and skills employees bring to their tasks, but the human mind and heart are hard to gauge. Still, companies need to tally up employee scorecards one way or another, not simply to maintain the status quo but as part of the process of developing new and improved practices for the future.

The performance of employee assets might be enhanced by making changes in the workplace environment, or in the compensation structure. Customer assets might be made more valuable by using data-mining techniques to unearth the information needed to forge more enduring relationships with customers.

British Airways offers an example of a company that has developed substantial new programs to enhance its employee assets, thereby also improving its customer relationships.[8]

Soon after British Airways was privatized in the mid-1980s, the airline, which has 300 aircraft flying to 170 destinations in more than 80 countries, recognized that it had to find ways to differentiate the quality of its service in the increasingly competitive airline industry. The skills and behaviors of its employees, the company's leaders decided, represented one of the few areas in which it might achieve that goal. Given its international clientele, British Airways had good reason to pay close attention to the attitudes and sensitivities of its employees.

Reservations agents, for example, had to understand that Indian men don't want their spouses sitting next to unknown males. Cabin attendants had to learn not to close food drawers with their feet, an offense to Thai travelers.

To bring its workforce up to international speed and improve interaction between employees and customers, BA has made major changes in its training and employee-relations programs. A symbol of BA's com-

British Airways reinvented its training and employee-relations program—enhancing the value of its employee and customer assets.

mitment to its goal can be found at Waterside, its new headquarters in London, where the emphasis is on providing workers with information they can use at work and in furthering their careers.

At Quest Centre, the company's on-site university, employees can participate in a wide variety of educational offerings, including a masters program in business administration and a degree in supervisory management. Every employee there has access to a multimedia personal computer geared for computer-based training.

BA also operates a continuing series of customer-service training programs, based upon research in the behavioral sciences, about how to relate to people, work on teams, and manage stress.

On another front, the company has set up special services to ease the lives of its far-flung cabin crews. For example, dry-cleaning facilities are provided for the crews at every airport served by the airline.

By adopting a portfolio strategy that called for a reinvented training and employee-relations program, British Airways increased the value of its employee assets, enhancing its customer assets and entire economic profile.

Strategy: **Connect**

Some messages are repeated so often we tend to forget what they really mean. How many times have members of a football team, for example, or salespeople at a regional meeting, heard leaders proclaim that a chain is only as strong as its weakest link?

The real point of the cliché, of course, is that every link in a chain—and every member of a team—is, at some level, involved with and dependent upon all the other elements. The hip bone is connected to the thigh bone, as the old song says.

Imagine the potential of pursuing a connect strategy in the professional-services industry, whereby one company distributes to customers not only its own product and service offerings, but also those of its competitors.

Charles Schwab has pursued that connect strategy. It reached beyond the ranks of retail customers to stockbrokers when it decided to move into the management of initial public offerings. Schwab also connected its own services to customers via the Internet and then expanded that forum of exchange to make it possible for everyone—its customers and its competitors' customers—to sample both its own and those same competitors' offerings on its Web site. That proved to be a brilliant connect strategy.

Compaq Computer Corporation's acquisition of Digital Equipment Corporation is another portfolio strategy that connected assets. On January 26, 1998, with a single maneuver, the company reinvented itself by dramatically restructuring its portfolio of assets. In the computer industry's biggest takeover to date, Compaq paid $9.6 billion for Digital, based in Maynard, Maryland.

In short order, Compaq's connect portfolio strategy became evident. It aligned the assets of the two companies by making the Compaq product offerings available to Digital's customer base and by making Digital's big sales-and-service force accessible to all Compaq's corporate customers.

In one fell swoop, Compaq went from manufacturing and selling products (single events) to long-term corporate relationships based on service offerings (multiple events). The result: Compaq increased the breadth and depth of its product line and its customer base.

Strategy: **Convert**

Sometimes creating new value requires something more drastic than enhancing the functionality of an asset or connecting one asset with another.

Sometimes you need to actually alter an asset's existing function—say, by turning it to a financial asset such as cash—or you have to dispose of a nonperforming asset altogether. This is the portfolio strategy we call conversion.

Examples abound. Consider the plight faced these days by many hospitals, which find themselves burdened with unfilled and unfillable extra beds. One conversion strategy adopted by some hospitals involves giving the unused areas a different purpose—as an outpatient wing, for example. In another conversion strategy, some hospitals are simply selling their excess space and using the cash to make the most of their remaining assets.

Consider the problem encountered by John T. Chambers, chairman and chief executive officer of Cisco Systems, Inc., when he decided to remake the company into a full-service provider. The substantial technical capabilities needed to accomplish his goal were not present in-house. His solution: He converted the increased value of Cisco's stock, offering shares to buy companies that had the required staff and expertise.

In effect, Cisco adopted a conversion strategy that turned financial assets—in the form of high-priced stock—into employee assets.

The next challenge was to extend the skills and experience of those employees to generate organization assets—that is, to use them to create know-how and intellectual property for the continuing benefit of the organization as a whole. (A key performance indicator for many companies today is the number of patents they obtain.)

The final step is the conversion of the intellectual property derived into income by licensing or selling it to the outside world.

In sum, the Cisco example is about applying a conversion strategy that transmutes financial assets to employee assets to organization assets and back to financial assets, as defined in the Value Dynamics Framework.

Strategy: Block

One of the secrets to the success of Dell Computer Corporation, as we discussed previously, has been its insistence upon controlling and minimizing its inventory. The advantages of that strategy are many, including the blocking effect it has on its competitors.

When the cost of raw materials drops substantially, companies that hold large inventories have a hard time matching the price cuts offered by competitors like Dell, with its small inventories.

Similarly, when a new technology appears, low-inventory businesses like Dell are able to retool more rapidly than their high-inventory rivals.

As Michael Dell once told a reporter, "If I've got 11 days of inventory and my competitor has 80, and Intel comes out with a new 450-mega-hertz chip, that means I'm going to get to market 69 days sooner."

It also means that Dell avoids the nightmare of a bursting-at-the-seams warehouse, which often forces companies to sell off their excess inventory at bargain-basement prices.

Dell's ability to constantly reduce its inventory dramatically lowers the company's costs. But, as Michael Dell suggests, it has another outcome that is a central consideration in developing a company's asset

> **Dell's ability to constantly reduce its inventory dramatically lowers the company's costs — and puts rivals at a disadvantage.**

strategy: It is a blocking strategy, putting Dell's rivals at a significant disadvantage.

Blocking moves are typically part of a two-fold strategy. We make the most of our assets not only to generate wealth for our organizations but also to place obstacles in the path of competitors, large and small. When we enter new markets or improve operational efficiency, we put impediments in the way of our rivals' use of their assets.

In other words, the Wal-Marts and the Southwest Airlines of the world guarantee an overall level of operational performance that raises the bar high enough to dishearten potential rivals. At the same time, it allows them to hold their own, or even increase, market share.

Or think about Coca-Cola and Pepsi, both masters of the blocking strategy, exploiting their brands with massive international advertising. Even Virgin—which has been able to take advantage of its strong brand name to enter many different markets—has failed to make significant inroads with its Virgin Cola.

By raising the stakes to astronomical levels, the leaders make it next to impossible for a would-be competitor to think about challenging them in the global marketplace.

▶ What's next?

The stakes are high in the New Economy. Companies have immense opportunity to create value during a time of rapid change. But, as we've noted, risk is inseparable from value creation for companies breaking the constraints of the past.

For many companies, breaking free requires a change of mind-set and a willingness to take on and manage more risk. In the next chapter, we address the challenge of mastering risk in the New Economy.

Ask Yourself:

■ What tangible and intangible assets are you using in your business? How has your company's business model changed in the last five years as a result of new strategies and asset investments?

■ Draw a Value Image to show roughly how your company currently allocates its resources across the five Value Dynamics asset classes. Now draw a Value Image of where your company wants to derive value in the next five years. What changes in your company's asset investments and strategies are required to achieve your goals?

■ How does your company use technology assets to enhance the value of its portfolio? Does it scale assets to maximize their value? How?

■ How might your company create value with the five generic asset-portfolio strategies (build, connect, enhance, convert, or block)? What other asset strategies might you employ?

■ Can you see ways that your competitors are using portfolio strategies to position themselves in the marketplace?

Master Risk.

"The
revolutionary
idea that defines
the boundary
between modern
times and the past
is the mastery of
risk. . . ."

-- Peter L. Bernstein[1]

"We are all paid to take risks," says Lawrence A. Bossidy, the former storied chairman and chief executive officer of AlliedSignal, Inc., the New Jersey-based maker of aerospace equipment and auto parts, once told *Fortune*.[2]

When he was 12 years old and an altar boy at St. Theresa's Church in Pittsfield, Massachusetts, Bossidy started helping out in his father's shoe store on evenings and weekends. He could barely reach the cash register, but he was a full-fledged salesman. He noted the everyday risks his father took in ordering some styles of shoes—and not ordering others.

A few years later, when a snowstorm swept in on a Friday night, his father gave Bossidy $500 in cash, and the young man drove to a midnight auction in another town. There, he practiced a kind of homespun risk management, buying dozens of pairs of galoshes on the assumption that enough snow would fall to produce a seller's market the next day.

Not all risk management can be reduced to an equation as simple as making a calculated decision that it will snow enough to drive up demand in galoshes. But the general principles remain the same.

Companies that alter their business models in response to the New Economy are taking risks, to be sure. But so are companies that elect to do nothing but stick with the tried-and-true.

The difference is, companies that respond proactively to the new business realities are likely to have a much better understanding of the risks they are taking than those companies that choose to do nothing in the mistaken belief they are avoiding risk. Above all, companies that redesign their business models understand that a new business model is as much about upside opportunity as downside threat.

Example: Andrew Grove, chairman of Intel Corporation, refers to risk as "points of inflection," or "the moment that massive change occurs and all bets are off."[3] Not surprisingly, he is putting Intel's future on the line with a $5-billion investment in the Internet. Grove has also announced a $100-million fund intended as seed money for companies that will create the communications networks of the future. Believing that data transmission will soon dominate voice in the networked economy, Grove is ready to go head-to-head with entrenched competitors.

Example: John F. Welch, Jr., chairman and chief executive officer of the General Electric Company, is betting $1 billion to $2 billion that the emerging Chinese economy, home to almost 20 percent of the world's potential consumers, will become a power in the global marketplace. Under Welch's leadership, GE is managing strategic risk by taking specific action to align its portfolio of assets with the changing world economy.

These companies are facing head-on the second challenge on the Value Dynamics agenda: Master risk in an uncertain environment.

To what are these smart leaders responding? What risks are they managing? And what asset-portfolio strategies are they using to manage the downside while enhancing the upside?

As the speed of change accelerates and a networked global economy creates opportunities of unprecedented scale, new risks are emerging. Industries are consolidating and converging. Unseen competitors are challenging mainline businesses. Business models are becoming obsolete. And traditional barriers between companies are breaking down, along with the "tried and true" human-based, "detect and correct" controls often put in place to reduce risk.

In today's world, companies need to capitalize on emerging market realities, rather than just playing out the cards they hold. You can't create a business that doesn't take risks. If you try, you will create a business that doesn't make money.

We have found it useful to define business risk in three broad groups to better understand the types of risks that businesses face. Without a framework, everyone starts with a "blank sheet of paper" every time they confront the subject of risk. Our firm's Business Risk Model (Figure 11.1) defines three categories of risk:

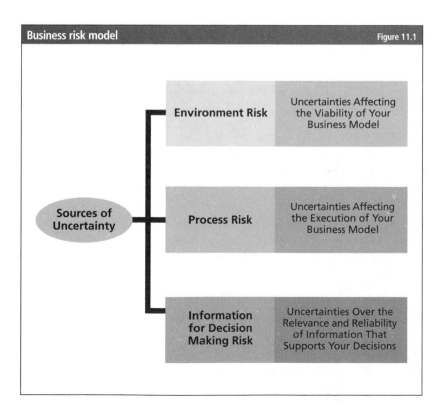

Business risk model   Figure 11.1

Sources of Uncertainty

Environment Risk — Uncertainties Affecting the Viability of Your Business Model

Process Risk — Uncertainties Affecting the Execution of Your Business Model

Information for Decision Making Risk — Uncertainties Over the Relevance and Reliability of Information That Supports Your Decisions

■ Environment risks affect the viability of your business model—that is, your overall asset portfolio decisions. Environment risks are most relevant to the first challenge on the Value Dynamics agenda: Design your business model for value creation. Examples of environment risks include changes in competitor capabilities, regulation and deregulation, financial markets volatility, political trends, and demographic/cultural shifts. What sets these risks apart is that they are usually beyond your ability to control. That is why your business model is vital; it helps you manage the impact of change in the key environment risk factors on your business.

■ Process risks affect your ability to implement your business model successfully. They are most relevant to the third challenge on the Value Dynamics path to creating value: Manage your asset portfolio. These types of risk increase as processes become obsolete, and new processes must be adopted to respond to the needs of new business models. Process risks apply to all aspects of acquiring, developing, managing and disposing of all of the assets in your portfolio.

■ Information for decision-making risks relate to every aspect of value creation. These risks particularly involve the fourth challenge of Value Dynamics: Use information to create value. Both the need for and the availability of information have made exponential leaps in the New Economy.

Before going further, let's reiterate a point made earlier. People often speak colloquially about risk as an adverse event or loss to be mitigated or insured against. We are speaking of risk in a much broader sense, however, which includes the unprecedented opportunity in the New Economy. For example, as a business person with a new idea, you could conceivably join the ranks of Bill Gates. On the other hand, you could also go bankrupt.

Risk, then, encompasses the uncertainty of future reward in terms of both the upside and the downside. And opportunity in business arises from managing the future. Companies today must face (and manage) the future knowing that they cannot simply carry on with business as usual. Over time, the old sources of wealth will simply disappear. Doing nothing is fraught with danger.

Today, as in ages past, unseen competitors from outside a particular industry are driving change for mainstream companies. The railroad barons, for instance, failed to see the devastating competition brought on by the birth of the auto industry or the airlines. In more recent times, makers of typewriters and analog watches saw their markets collapse under the weight of new technology.

Even the likes of Microsoft can stumble by failing to give full attention to technological change. The giant software maker underestimated the importance of the Internet, letting Netscape seize an early lead in this market with the Navigator browser it gave away to users.

High future returns don't automatically translate into great value. That's because value has two elements—risk and return.

Strategy today is all about setting a course within this unpredictable environment. Mastering risk means designing a business model, and making it work through effective and efficient processes supported by relevant and reliable information.

Make no mistake, the rewards for successful pioneers can be enormous. In fact, a growing number of adventurous entrepreneurs are joining the ranks of newly minted millionaires and billionaires in today's economic milieu.

But there is a catch.

High future returns don't automatically translate into great value today, especially when those returns are uncertain and all in the future. That's because value has two elements—risk and return.

Although return is often equated with earnings and profits, these are just indicators of what really matters in terms of value realization, namely cash flow. Markets value the equity of companies on the basis of what their projected future cash flow is worth today. But future cash flow is uncertain, especially for equity owners, who reap benefits from their investment only after all other claims are met.

When future cash flows are risk-free, the cost of capital, reflected in the discount rate applied to those cash flows, is at its lowest, and the present value of the cash flow is at its highest. The more uncertain those cash flows are, the more heavily they are discounted and the less they are worth.

A simple example: A cash flow stream resulting from a $100 million bond would be discounted at the stated rate of interest (say 6.5 percent) to give it a present value equivalent to the bond's face amount, assuming its owner intends to hold it until maturity and the financial wherewithal of the issuer is beyond question or "risk-free" (such as with U.S. treasuries).

In contrast, the cash flow stream from a business is uncertain as to both amount and timing. For one thing, the amount of the annual cash flows cannot be predicted with absolute certainty, even a year into the future. For another, the timeframe over which the income stream is discounted is a function of its predictability, approaches customary to the industry, and the investor's appetite for projecting into the future. To address these risks, the rate used to discount future cash flows reflects a risk premium above and beyond the risk-free rate. The greater the premium for risk, the less the present value of the projected cash flow streams, of course.

Two separate issues—the reality and the perception—must be dealt with if you expect to master risk. Here's what we mean.

If investors aren't confident that a company can master risk in what looks to be a chancy endeavor, they are likely to further discount the value they attribute to the company's stock. So mastering risk is about more than just attaining better economic outcomes. It is also about soothing skittish investors.

In other words, value is in the eye of the investor. Effective communication of risk-management strategies can change the perception (and value) of your company in the marketplace.

Companies thus need a forward-looking, proactive, and systematic process for evaluating risk and reward. As the song goes, you can't have one without the other. So too with strategic planning and risk management.

Given that reality, let's look at examples of how three companies manage the types of risk we've identified in our model.

Q: Who is managing risks arising from change in the environment?

A: Merrill Lynch & Company, Inc.

In an earlier chapter, we explored how customer assets have promoted the astonishing rise of Charles Schwab. Here's another question: Who could have guessed that Merrill Lynch, the long-time leader in financial services in the investment field, would fall behind in the realm of direct, Web-based services to investors?

It is a question that takes on a different cast in light of our discussion of risk. Now we must ask: How can Merrill Lynch respond strategically to the environment risk caused by new market competitors that are

How can companies use new technologies to change the ratio of risk and reward?

using new technologies? What changes in its business model are required to preserve its competitiveness? How can the company use the newest technologies to increase its customer and supply-chain assets, changing the ratio of risk and reward both for itself and for competitors—including those who have the first-mover advantage?

It is now clear that Merrill's network of brokers and branch officers became less valuable as on-line trading mushroomed. In other words, the marketplace produced risk that Merrill delayed in addressing. Indeed, published reports now reveal that it took a highly publicized internal battle before the company finally bowed to the inevitable, the redesign of its business model.[4] Suggestive of the boardroom attitudes was a comment by Chairman David Komansky that if a "bunch of yuppies could attract investors on the Internet, so, too, could Merrill Lynch."[5]

The argument for change was persuasive. Though Merrill managed $500 billion, its customer assets more directly belonged to its brokers, not the company. On the other hand, Schwab, as a firm, has access to and information about all of its millions of customers. It also has access to information about each of the members of its supply chain, which is the key to its extraordinary "one source" offering.

In mid-1999, Merrill Lynch announced that it would establish Internet trading at a discounted fee of $29.95 per trade. But that only hints at the radical nature of the change in business model that Merrill made virtually overnight. It is a model that will change Merrill's relationship with its 14,000 brokers, once the foundation on which its business was built.

Now that giant Merrill has taken the plunge, other full-service Wall Street brokerage firms may follow its lead into on-line trading and customer acquisition. Traditional brokers will not be able to hold back the tide as the Internet and related technologies change the competitive landscape. These companies will need to manage a portfolio of risk that has changed dramatically because of market conditions.

Nor will the on-line financial services revolution stop there. On the same day that Merrill announced its plans for on-line trading, E*TRADE Group, Inc., the global provider of personal electronic financial services headquartered in Menlo Park, California, disclosed the nearly $2-billion acquisition of Telebanc Financial Corporation, of Arlington, Virginia, the national on-line bank. Thus, the on-line industry is consolidating just as the off-line world has done.

It is not our intention to single out Merrill Lynch for criticism informed by hindsight—the dramatic changes inspired by the New Economy have caught many business managers unaware. The status quo is outdated quickly in a dynamic environment in which companies relentlessly seek to "leapfrog" over their competitors with new strategies. Environment risks are increasing and any company—even the best and brightest—is vulnerable. You need to assess which assets are your best competitive weapons and stay ahead of the risks.

Let's move on to another type of risk—arising not from the environment, but from the ways businesses operate and make decisions. Specifically, a company's portfolio of risks also includes process risk, the second category outlined in our Business Risk Model.

It's our view that the degree of process risk a company encounters is determined by how it manages its asset portfolio—that is, how it acquires, manages, renews, and disposes of assets. To put it another way, businesses incur process risk as they implement and execute a business model.

Q: Who is managing processes to master business risk?
A: The Gillette Company.

Two decades ago, when managers at the Gillette Company saw that disposable razors were eroding the company's market share, they were dismayed. For generations, the name Gillette had been synonymous with quality razors the world over, and the maker of personal and household products was determined to protect its brand and market share.[6]

In short order, after a huge investment in the manufacture and marketing of the new products, Boston-based Gillette became the king of the disposables. But the company wore its crown uneasily.

Competition in disposables was strictly on the basis of price. Aside from the fact that this commodity market yielded—if you will excuse the pun—razor-thin margins, Gillette's leaders began to feel that they had taken the company in the wrong direction. They wanted to return to the days when the Gillette name evoked, first and foremost, quality, which in turn produced customer loyalty.

Back to the future: The company decided to reinvent not only the business model, but the company's processes, too. In 1989, Gillette, headed by new chairman and chief executive officer Alfred Zeien,

> **Gillette's new strategy required the company to manage process risk related to developing and marketing new, upscale razor technology.**

stopped promoting its disposable razors. At the same time, it started beating the drum for a new upscale product, the Sensor, with a slogan that captured the corporate change of heart: "The Best a Man Can Get."

At the center of this story is a willingness to take risks, which inherently carries the possibility of failure (or success). Obviously the company could not have known for certain that developing a new high-quality razor would reap benefits. In putting the Sensor at the heart of its future, Gillette was responding in part to its competitive position, that is, its environment risk.

But the series of decisions made by Gillette also required the company to master process risk, beginning with the research and development of a new, upscale razor technology. In addition, the company had to mobilize its brand management and marketing processes to reposition its message, focusing on razor quality, not price.

By year-end 1999, Gillette had a market capitalization of $44.2 billion, a nine-fold increase over a decade before. The company and its shareholders benefited when Gillette opted to incur process risk by redirecting its business toward a new market opportunity. In sum, Gillette effectively aligned its processes to execute the new business model and strategy, which were themselves designed to respond to changing external realities. This is the essence of managing process risk.

Now we turn to the third source of risk: information for decision-making, which is at the heart of New Economy challenges.

In their own way, financial institutions have always been specialists in risk management, because the assumption of risk is the essence of their business. Over the years, they have developed ever more sophisticated risk-management capabilities. The rigor and science of their techniques can enhance business opportunity and provide a source of best practices for industrial companies, too.

Q: Who is mastering information for decision-making risk?
A: Chase Manhattan Bank.

Until 1997, Chase's risk-management model assumed that there were specific limits to the liability the bank might encounter—limits determined by developing remote worst-case scenarios. That was the year when Chase incurred some hefty losses in Latin America and seemed about to hit those limits. Although the actual losses of $100 million were substantially lower, the experience led Chase to undertake an all-out effort to evaluate, measure, monitor, and manage risk even more effectively.

Chase put its loan and trading portfolios under the magnifying glass. So-called stress tests were devised—based on real nightmares like the 1987 crash on Wall Street—to determine how the different elements of the portfolios would respond to disaster and to estimate the risk. Chase now applies up to 10 such scenarios to its hundreds of thousands of trading positions monthly.[7]

The payoff from Chase's preparations came when Russia's currency collapsed in the summer of 1998, and investors moved suddenly from stocks to bonds. Although Chase's crystal-ball gazers had not actually predicted the Russian debacle, they had devised and applied a stress test that simulated a flight from stocks to bonds. As a result, Chase was able to weather the blow better than most of its competitors.

Chase leads the banking industry in extending its risk-management techniques deep into the heart of its organization. It does more than

> ## IT permitted Chase to change the basic premise of risk management. Chase can now find out what customers themselves want and need.

look at financial risk. Chase also looks at asset risks, like those that stem from acquiring new customers, serving existing customers, and finding ways to deepen relationships with them.

Donald L. Boudreau, vice chairman of Chase, compares customer risk management before and after information technology arrived. "It was almost like throwing millions of pieces of direct mail or in-branch brochures up against a wall," he says, "and hoping that some of it stuck . . . and then, of course, hoping that the ones that stuck were the customers you really wanted, namely creditworthy and profitable."[8]

Today, Chase can tap into vast quantities of computer-accessible data and predict "almost anything" in terms of customer risk and reward. Boudreau says Chase can now accurately forecast the likelihood that a customer will accept a specific product offering or value package, refinance a mortgage, or leave the company for a competitor. It can even suggest the price point needed to prevent that customer from leaving. In other words, Chase has come up with a way to determine when its assets are losing value—one customer at a time.

In the past the bank's sales efforts had to be based on the averages, which were dependent on groupings of customers and thus tended to hide individual differences. The risks were inevitable and substantial, and Boudreau admits to some "costly errors in decision making." Today, the company's information-based business system reduces that risk.

Each and every experience a customer has with the bank is immediately made part of the person's electronic record. That data is used to develop a prediction of the customer's value to the organization—what Chase calls lifetime net present value. The electronic record is accessible on the desktop or laptop computers of Chase sales and marketing employees, whom the bank calls relationship managers. That record means that customers never have to reintroduce themselves.

It also means that the bank's relationship managers can suggest solutions based upon the pattern of the customer's past preferences, both as to product and service channel. They can use the data to decide whether to offer an upgrade to a better product and for cross-selling in general.

And all these decisions can be made quickly and easily by a relationship manager sitting with a laptop in a customer's home or office.

The uses of information-based business systems are infinite. For example, it allows Chase to identify customers who are inclined to refinance a loan, screen out those with a low economic value to the company, and approach the remainder with an offer. The system's predictive skills have also been used to reduce losses stemming from credit card fraud.

Having that ability has gone a long way toward reducing risk throughout the organization. Whether it is testing loans or second-guessing customers, Chase has found ways to put its risk management to work in addressing all five of the Value Dynamics asset classes. As Chase well knows, risk management has to cover all the assets—and it can't stop at the corporate boundary line. It must extend into the marketplace. Information creates the bridge.

How do you become a master of risk? Companies need to learn how their investments in assets create exposures to both an upside and a downside. Many managers think of risk only in terms of tangible assets. But intangible sources of value are often the greatest source of risk. In short, you need to look at risks systematically in terms of old economy and New Economy assets. Installing inventory management systems, for example, was once cutting-edge, but is now a routine way to manage these process risks. Risk management issues of the old economy don't go away. They simply become the "ante" to be in the game.

Risk-reward profiles for the most valuable assets of the New Economy are where improvement is required and competitive edge can be gained. In fact, we recommend that companies go through an exercise to identify old and New Economy risks within the three broad categories we identified (environment, process, and information for decision-making).

Risks need to be clearly identified, the sources pinpointed, or root causes measurement and monitoring processes set up.

Success in mastering risk, as a result, requires companies to systematically broaden capabilities in risk management. This means effectively combining processes, people, technology, and knowledge for the purpose

> ## Companies need to learn how investments in assets create exposures to both the upside and downside. And intangibles may be the greatest source of risk of all.

of achieving the company's strategies. Simply stated, if you don't have a deliberate process for designing and implementing the capabilities you need, then risk management won't occur. Just as a company needs a process for paying its bills or delivering goods to its customers, it needs a systematic way to manage risk.

Your company has many options for managing its individual and groups of related risks. For example, you can avoid, retain, reduce, transfer, and exploit risk.

Consider risk avoidance first. The options include divesting of businesses and prohibiting or restricting specific activities. Your business model provides a powerful context for this assessment, as a desirable risk is one that is inherent in that model.

Risk retention results in accepting risk at its present level. It may involve various forms of captives and self-insurance to fund losses if they occur. It also includes the use of deductibles and the aggregation of risks for offsetting within well-defined portfolios.

Risk reduction strategies reduce the severity of the risk and/or its likelihood of occurrence. For example, risk control processes reduce the likelihood that an undesirable event will occur; once implemented, these processes must be assessed continuously to ensure that they are performing as intended.

Risk transfer options incorporate the use of hedging and insurance to provide a form of contingent capital. While fees and premiums do reduce earnings, the risk transfer that hedging or insurance contracts make possible enable you to operate with a lower level of economic capital than you would otherwise need.

Risk exploitation strategies are used to enter new markets, introduce new products, merge with or acquire another firm or exploit other market opportunities, all of which reshape a company's risk profile. Companies can exploit risk through diversification, expansion, arbitrage, and other approaches.

Keep in mind that when taking on risks to exploit market opportunities, each company has areas where it excels relative to its competitors. (For example, your company may have a substantially lower average cost of managing a particular risk as compared to competitors.) The most successful companies exploit these advantages to maximum effect. Conversely, you will want to avoid exposure to those areas that are not consistent with your company's competencies or which management considers "off-strategy."

Putting a focus on risk, however, without seeing it in the context of value creation is like viewing the world with one eye closed. You lose perspective, and risky opportunities are spurned. Risk management activities become fragmented and take on a life of their own. Risk controls outlive their original purpose. Risk strategies become obsolete.

Historically, risk management was directed at financial capital and fixed assets. Now, however, new sources of value produce new risks, often relating to assets that a company doesn't own or control, nor has measured as value creating. What does that mean for you? Your risk management needs to follow your market opportunities and strategy as you develop new business models.

When all is said and done, mastering risk to create value is about improving risk management capabilities continuously as the external and internal business realities change. Remember: Risk must be mastered if you want to be one of the success stories of the New Economy.

▶ What's next?

Anyone who has ever tried to make a soufflé knows that it is risky. Get it right, and you are the toast of the table. But the slightest mistake results in a red-faced chef.

Imagine that you are a restaurant owner who must decide whether to put soufflés on the menu. How will you manage the risks?

Value Dynamics suggests that you can master risk, in part, by asking the right questions. That's as true for General Motors as for a neighborhood restaurant. So as the owner of our mythical restaurant, you need to ask yourself a number of questions.

Will your customers even want soufflé (environment risk)? The restaurant must understand its customers and their preferences, and how many might be expected to dine on any given evening.

Does the chef have the recipe (information for decision-making) and the right people to create a soufflé and deliver it successfully to diners (process risk)? Having the right number of waiters on hand is important, too, so the chef can get the orders in and out of the kitchen.

It is clear that making a soufflé and running a business can both be risky. The future is uncertain, but risk can be managed. Indeed, it must be managed if a company is to benefit from the opportunities of the New Economy.

To continue our analogy, the topic of our next chapter is how you as owner must manage the whole portfolio of your assets, from chefs to waiters, so that you can deliver the perfect soufflé to the table.

Ask Yourself:

- How is risk defined at your company? Is risk seen only in a negative light or is it also seen as including opportunity?

- What are your company's biggest risks in the three risk categories: environment, process, and information for decision making?

- Does your company connect strategy, risk management and value creation? If so, how?

- How is your company positioned to manage risk in the New Economy? Do you reward people who take risks and understand risk management?

- Is risk management a source of competitive advantage in your company or a cost center?

❑

Manage Your Asset Portfolio.

"Insistently, persistently, relentlessly, the new manager must ask, "What for?" What is it that we're in business for? What is this process for? This product? This task? This team? This job: What are we doing here, anyway?"

—James Champy

H ow did the Chicago Bulls become the winningest—and wealthiest—franchise in professional basketball history during the 1990s?

The Bulls legend had its start in 1984, when things were as bad as they could get for this mediocre team that had never won a National Basketball Association (NBA) championship. With thousands of seats to fill, the Bulls were barely able to attract 6,000 spectators per game at an average of $15 a seat.

But that year, by some stroke of luck or inspiration, the Bulls changed the course of their history. They acquired a genius, a basketball player skilled beyond compare and so airborne that he seemed to repeal the laws of gravity.

The $850,000 starting salary they paid the young guard from the University of North Carolina turned out to be a slam dunk. The basketball bargain of the century, Michael Jordan, transformed Chicago into a bastion of basketball pride and profit.

By the end of the 1998 season, attendance was up almost 120 percent, with 24,000 spectators a game willing and eager to pay an average of $30 a ticket.

The team's ownership—Jerry Reinsdorf—benefited mightily. The value of their franchise soared by 1,000 percent, from less than $20 million the year Jordan arrived to more than $200 million.

Under the management of head coach Phil Jackson, the Bulls won six NBA championships in eight years. Late in Jordan's career, the team rewarded its star player accordingly, with a salary of more than $33 million a year.

But what about the Chicago Bulls, Inc.? How did the franchise create value for itself? It didn't sell tickets or park cars. It didn't employ the roving beer and hot-dog vendors. It didn't operate the scoreboard, much less run the arena.

The long answer: It was the management of assets—although mostly intangible assets—that made the difference. It was the players and coaches, systems and processes, leadership and values, customers and suppliers. Most of the team's revenues, in fact, came not from ticket sales

The Bulls management built a portfolio of assets that created extraordinary wealth.

but from everything else—broadcast licensing fees, use of the Bulls logo on T-shirts and hats, and other methods of making the most of the Bulls brand.

The short answer: The Bulls management built value with a portfolio of assets that was specifically designed to create and realize extraordinary wealth.

But situations change. People move on. Asset values shift. The Bulls' value-creating formula changed with the team's struggle to arrive at a "new beginning" when Coach Jackson's resigned, Jordan retired, and free-agent Scottie Pippen and bad-boy rebounder Dennis Rodman left the Bulls.

Some observers argue that management's decisions turned seemingly unlimited value creation into losses for the team and its associated sponsors—Nike and the NBA.

The Bulls management, however, might maintain that their key player assets—Jordan, Pippin, and Rodman—were aging and nearing retirement, and that it was time to let them go and invest in the next generation of assets.

In any event, determining whether the Bulls management made the right decisions is not our intent here. Our concern is with the deliberate and systematic process, by which organizations manage portfolios of assets for value creation.

And there is a lesson to be learned from the Bulls experience: Successful companies—even star-studded sports franchises—manage their businesses as a portfolio of assets, using their understanding of key asset management processes to enable and prolong their organizations' success. That is, they acquire, manage, renew, and dispose of individual assets in ways designed to create value for the portfolio as a whole.

In this chapter, we explore the third challenge for creating value in the New Economy: Manage your business as a portfolio of assets.

The methods used for managing an asset portfolio are, we believe, among the underlying forces that drive value creation. Designing a robust business model is critical, but companies must also execute well. Companies acquire individual assets in the asset portfolio, deploy and renew them, and then dispose of them. They compete in the marketplace based on these portfolio decisions and the business processes used to implement them.

To make the right decisions, managers need to recognize that every asset, both tangible and intangible, has a life cycle. That life cycle is based on the asset's economic life—in contrast to its functional or locational life. In other words, nothing lasts forever. An asset's economic life has a distinct beginning, middle, and end.

Buildings are constructed or acquired, managed, renovated, and eventually torn down. Computer equipment is purchased, used, sometimes upgraded, and finally consigned to the basement. Customers are acquired, relationships managed, new solutions developed, until eventually they depart for other product or service offerings. Employees are recruited, managed, trained, and re-deployed, but, ultimately, they leave.

The list doesn't stop there. Everyone has worked with companies whose culture or other organization assets have grown stagnant through lack of investment and renewal. Every asset can be acquired, managed, renewed, disposed of or destroyed.

Assets Have Life Cycles:

Example: Fixed assets. The concept "location, location, location" was paramount in the commercial real estate market when local stores controlled retailing. But that sacrosanct notion was turned on its head by the Internet. This virtual portal to the consumer created a new kind of extra-physical location for bringing businesses and customers together.

Example: Technologies. The telephone companies strung wires up and down city streets and across the prairies to bring the miracle of the telegraph and then voice communication to the public. One miracle was superseded by another, however, and suddenly satellites and cellular systems were threatening the value of the companies' telephone poles. Internet telephony and other future technologies can be expected to dramatically realign values yet again, renewing the value of some assets and making others redundant.

Example: Employees. The value of human assets changes, too, as many companies and employees have discovered. How many auto companies spent years training employees to give them the skills needed to build cars on assembly lines, only to discover that jobs were changing and the number of employees required was shrinking? On the employee side of the equation, many auto workers discovered that the jobs created in the changing economy required workers with different sets of skills. The reality is that new technologies have accelerated the pace of hiring, training, and losing employees.

Example: Customers. Retailers strive constantly to reinvent their offerings in order to acquire and build relationships with demanding customers, but the life cycle of customer assets has been shrinking. Too much product, the result of production efficiencies, is chasing too few customers. Today, customers are in the driver's seat. Information technology advances have made them much better informed of their choices and less likely to settle for second best. Customer loyalty has diminished.

> **Example: Business models.** Economic change can vastly reduce the life cycle of business models, and change is the order of our day. Vertically integrated companies have often failed to recognize that fact. Utilities in the United States, for example, have historically controlled the generation, distribution, and trading of power. But some management groups didn't know where the real value was being created along that supply chain—and the protective regulatory environment provided no incentive for them to find out. Then came deregulation, and the value chain for the electric utilities began to fragment. Niche competitors emerged that could manage particular segments of the value chain better than the utilities—and could manage risk better, as well. Now, the old-line utilities are seeing their economies of scale disintegrate. Our view is that new business models are emerging in that industry.

Managing asset life cycles, as a result, comes down to knowing how and when to acquire, manage, renew, and shed an asset—all the assets that create the value of a business. And the key to timing is in the marketplace. Heed market signals about the value of your assets, and align your portfolio accordingly.

All business processes can be classified within the context of these basic life cycle portfolio actions. Acquiring customers, for example, includes a range of marketing and promotion activities. Acquiring, managing, renewing, and disposing of supply-chain partners involves contractual processes and performance arrangements.

The New Economy has created many new business models (e.g., Dell's "Be Direct"), technologies (e.g., Internet infrastructure) and new alliances (e.g., outsourcing). In turn, these changes have altered industries, produced new products and services, and dramatically changed how value is created.

But don't forget: The fundamental business processes are also important as a source of value creation. Value is created in every business model—across the entire asset portfolio—through basic business processes and individual work activities. An understanding of these business processes is critical to managing what matters.

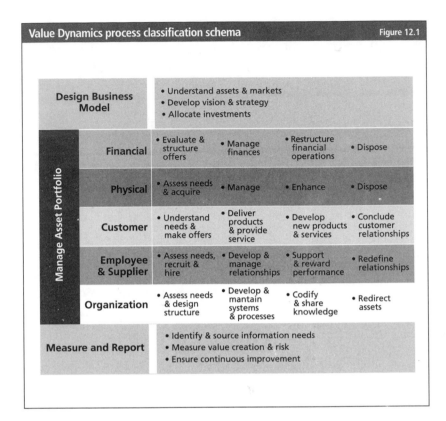

Value Dynamics process classification schema   Figure 12.1

Design Business Model		• Understand assets & markets • Develop vision & strategy • Allocate investments			
Manage Asset Portfolio	**Financial**	• Evaluate & structure offers	• Manage finances	• Restructure financial operations	• Dispose
	Physical	• Assess needs & acquire	• Manage	• Enhance	• Dispose
	Customer	• Understand needs & make offers	• Deliver products & provide service	• Develop new products & services	• Conclude customer relationships
	Employee & Supplier	• Assess needs, recruit & hire	• Develop & manage relationships	• Support & reward performance	• Redefine relationships
	Organization	• Assess needs & design structure	• Develop & mantain systems & processes	• Codify & share knowledge	• Redirect assets
Measure and Report		• Identify & source information needs • Measure value creation & risk • Ensure continuous improvement			

Figure 12.1 represents the Value Dynamics process classification system, which integrates processes relating to the four challenges of strategy, risk management, asset management, and information.

None of these basic business processes is new, and the process structure, by itself, may look simply theoretical. What is new and, we believe, compelling, is seeing these processes as dynamic drivers of excellence in each asset category, understanding how the processes of each major asset group contribute to your business model, and gaining insight into how the processes should interact to support the total business model.

To bring these processes to life, you need to start with a careful analysis of what asset groups are most important to the success of your business model and how existing processes are contributing to that goal. You must be willing to be disturbed by emerging best practices of other companies, and to make changes to processes to invigorate value creation. This is the essence of managing your asset portfolio, and it is essential to success in the New Economy.

To show how some best practices companies manage their asset portfolios in the real world, let's look at examples for each of the stages of the asset life cycle. We begin by looking at how two technology companies acquire assets, and in so doing create immense amounts of value.

Q: Who is creating value by acquiring customer assets?
A: LinkExchange, Inc. and Microsoft Corporation.

LinkExchange, Inc., an Internet upstart in San Francisco, had just one goal when it was founded in March 1996 by Tony Hsieh and Sanjay Madan, two Harvard alumni: to help Web-based clients acquire customers by advertising on other Web sites. LinkExchange earned a fee for brokering the deals that connected Web-site owners with one another.[1]

A year and a half later, after proving itself a master in customer acquisition, the company's initial staff of 10 had grown to 100, and it was receiving venture capital funding from Sequoia Capital, the same firm that had invested in Yahoo!, Inc. (itself a master in the leveraging of customer assets).

More than 800,000 customers used one or more of LinkExchange's services to increase traffic and build on-line revenues. Its Web sites reached more than 21 million on-line users. Its clients included the likes of American Airlines, Disney, Microsoft, Procter & Gamble, Universal Studios, and Yahoo!

But the story doesn't end there.

Waiting in the wings was Microsoft Corporation, which was seeking to extend its presence in the arena. In the fall of 1998, Microsoft purchased LinkExchange for $265 million in common stock. Not a bad return for 32 months' work, and a lesson in the magical effect of acquiring active customers at a compounded rate made possible by the scalability of the Internet.

The tale of LinkExchange and Microsoft shows how rapidly customer assets can be acquired in the New Economy.

Q: Who is creating value by acquiring employee assets?

A: Cisco Systems, Inc.

Cisco Systems, Inc. is a success by any measure. And as it has grown, so has its need for a greatly enlarged and multi-talented workforce. Acquisitions have met part of that need, but the company has also been forced to battle for the best and brightest in the notoriously tight and competitive technology job market.

That Cisco has succeeded in that struggle, as evidenced by performance reviews of new employees and an amazingly low turnover rate, is a tribute to the company's decision to develop and maximize another of its processes—human capital acquisition, otherwise known as employee recruitment.

In 1997, Cisco doubled its workforce, to 8,000 employees. A large pro-

> ## Cisco's recruiters show up in the most unexpected places, including art fairs and microbrewery tastings.

portion of these new hires were top-notch engineers who were not even thinking about changing jobs until Cisco came knocking.

To find such people—and determine how best to approach them— the company set up focus groups comprised of employees whose qualities most closely approximated those of the targeted prospects. Group members were peppered with questions about everything from their most-bookmarked Web sites to their favorite free-time activities. Based on their answers, Cisco fashioned an ingenious, innovative recruiting process.

The company's recruiters show up in the most unexpected places, including art fairs and tastings at microbreweries. They also mingle with the crowds at the yearly home and garden show in Silicon Valley. The show is popular with targeted engineers who also happen to be in the market for plants and furniture to fix up their first-ever homes.

The company's Web site (www.cisco.com) is a powerful piece of the recruitment process. Help-wanted ads in newspapers simply direct readers to the site instead of presenting lists of available jobs. Once there, prospective employees can call up openings in their areas of expertise and read detailed job descriptions.

Potential hires can also sign up for the "Make Friends @ Cisco" program. This on-line matchmaker promises to "connect you with an employee who shares your career objective" and will answer questions such as "How do you feel about working at Cisco?" and "What's the culture like?"

The idea for the make-friends program came from focus-group sessions at which participants were asked what could possibly lead them to look into job opportunities at another company. They said it would take the urging of a friend who claimed to have a better deal at his or her organization.

So Cisco volunteers talk on the phone with prospects who have similar backgrounds. If a prospect is hired, the volunteer friend receives $500 or more and a chance for an all-expense-paid trip to Hawaii.

Yet another improvement in the process allows prospective employees to build a relevant profile on the Cisco Web site in far less time than it would take to write and submit a resume. Instead of asking applicants to fill in blanks with data about their interests and backgrounds, Cisco provides a series of pull-down menus for employment and educational data. Based on their selections, applicants are then asked a series of questions. Besides saving the applicant's time, the program makes the résumés easier to review.

Company leaders say the on-line approach has saved Cisco hundreds of millions of dollars in recruiting expenses. Not bad for a process used to acquire employee assets.

Acquisition is only the first process in the asset life cycle. Next up: Management of the individual pieces that create value for the business as a whole.

Q: Who is creating value by managing supplier assets?

A: Calyx & Corolla, Inc.

Founded by Ruth M. Owades, a 1975 graduate of the Harvard Business School, Calyx & Corolla, Inc., of San Francisco, ships flowers directly from the grower to the consumer as soon as they're picked. "Our flowers," Owades told *Catalog Age*, "don't take detours."[2]

Owades' fresh approach to the $13 billion-a-year business of selling flowers required her to set up a new supply-and-delivery system that affected not only her own operations but the operations and practices of her most important vendors as well.

Calyx & Corolla's commitment to delivering only the freshest flowers produced logistical challenges at both ends of the system. Unlike its competitors, who use local florists to fill orders, Calyx & Corolla eliminated middlemen and their slow route to delivery—often 5 to 10 days. The company, however, realized the vital role those local florists played in their competitors' transactions. To make its system work, Calyx had to persuade its suppliers—the growers—to assemble, arrange, and package individual bouquets instead of just shipping bulk.

Next, Calyx convinced air carrier FDX Corporation (a.k.a. Federal Express, based in Memphis, Tennessee) to work with the company. FedEx agreed to pick up directly from independent growers, rather than funneling their orders through a central warehouse.[2]

Calyx built a $20 million business by understanding how to leverage its suppliers, enriching the entire supply chain in the process.

The occasions that call for flowers—weddings, birthday parties, and Mother's Day, for example—often take place on weekends. But since the shipper already made Saturday deliveries, that was not an issue. Calyx did have to persuade FedEx to leave packages at unanswered doors. Calyx promised to assume liability, and FedEx agreed.

When all was said and done, what distinguished Calyx & Corolla from other companies was just this: It had an acute understanding of how to manage a string of suppliers, one of the core Value Dynamics asset classes. In the process, it enriched every company in the supply chain.

As a result of the management of its supplier assets, Calyx & Corolla is blossoming—and producing value. It buys flowers from 25 suppliers in California, Florida, and Hawaii, as well as in Australia, Holland, Singapore, Thailand, and New Zealand. Its revenues now top $20 million a year.

Q: Who is creating value by managing organization assets?
A: FDX Corporation.

On the face of it, you might think that the most important asset of the world's leading express-delivery company would be its delivery system made up of 600 aircraft and 40,000 vehicles. You would be wrong. FedEx recognized early that the future lay with its package-tracking system, so the company devised a long-term strategy to enhance this organization asset.[3]

It succeeded so well that the tracking system has become the company's single greatest competitive advantage worldwide. In fact, the tracking system is so efficient and reliable that many international corporations have hired FedEx to manage their inventory, warehousing, distribution, and customs clearance.

Farming out those duties enabled one such customer, National Semiconductor Corporation, to reduce its total logistics cost from 3 percent of revenues to 1.9 percent between 1993 and 1996.

The FedEx tracking system can electronically determine where any package is at any point of its journey. When the recipient signs a handheld device carried by the delivery person, the signature and the delivery information are automatically entered into the FedEx central tracking system.

FedEx further enhanced this asset by duplicating it on-line. The company established a Web site that enables a shipper or a recipient to

Federal Express turned its package-tracking system into one of the company's major advantages.

locate a package simply by typing in the package number. What is more, the customer can actually arrange for the entire transaction on-line—from placing the order to receiving word of its delivery—without paperwork or phone calls. FedEx has installed computer terminals for 100,000 customers and given proprietary software to another 650,000. More than two-thirds of the company's customers use the Web site.

These FedEx processes have succeeded so well, and have increased market value so greatly, that the company is thinking about spinning off its huge delivery system and focusing entirely on its information and tracking assets.

Viewed through the Value Dynamics lens, we see that Federal Express took a conventional package-tracking system and enhanced this process asset to make it into the company's single greatest competitive advantage worldwide. It sought to increase profitability not by reducing costs but by building and managing customer value.

Assets can also be renewed to create value. The next company we highlight did just that, much to the profit of its stakeholders.

Q: Who is creating value by renewing employee assets?
A: Mary Kay, Inc.

Mary Kay, Inc., is a perennial name on lists of the best organizations to work for in the United States. Headquartered in Dallas, Texas, this privately held cosmetics company has also found an intriguing way to renew its relationships with customers and employees.

Almost all Mary Kay salespeople start out as Mary Kay consumers. The advantages to the company are substantial. The salespeople know precisely what they are getting into. They have a keen insight into what customers need and want. They already know the company, have a good feel for what will be expected of them, and require relatively little training.

The end result is a crew of highly motivated and successful workers. And that turns out to be a self-perpetuating system, since good workers make customers more likely to volunteer to become workers themselves. If that isn't a case of asset renewal, what is?

Some 500,000 Mary Kay salespeople demonstrate the company's

> ## Some 500,000 Mary Kay salespeople demonstrate products to some 20 million customers.

products in small-group settings to some 20 million customers in the United States and 28 other countries. The company sells more than 135 million items a year in nine categories: facial skin care, color cosmetics, body care, fragrances, hair care, nail care, men's skin care, nutritional supplements, and sun-protection products.

Founded in 1963 by Mary Kay Ash—who used her life savings of $5,000—the company offers every employee an equal chance at success. Each and every consultant begins with the same $100 start-up kit of cosmetic products. Each buys directly from the company and pays the same price. Each has the same chance to move up through the various levels of responsibility: Team leader, team manager, director, senior director, national sales director. Currently, more than 8,500 women (and a few men, too) are Mary Kay directors. More than 100 people are sales directors, earning six-figure commissions annually.

In the end, everyone—company and consultants alike—gets to enjoy the value they create. With its system for continuously renewing relationships, Mary Kay posts sales of more than $1 billion a year.[4]

The fourth and final portfolio process is disposal. Disposing of an asset may look like nothing more than getting rid of a problem. But it's much more than that, as our next two examples show.

Q: Who is creating value by disposing of inventory assets?
A: Priceline.com.

An Internet retailer based in Stamford, Connecticut, priceline.com Inc., is the name-your-price Internet auction company. It links supplier assets with potential customer assets, and then uses today's tools to create a virtual auction market in a variety of products and services.[5]

Every day, consumers log on to priceline.com to purchase, at a discount, tickets for airline seats that would otherwise go empty. The airlines hope, in turn, that priceline.com will be able to sell all their excess capacity.

You may be wondering, where is the asset disposition process in this company's strategy? Simply put, priceline.com has formed an alliance with the airlines to dispose of their excess assets. In the process, it becomes a part of their yield-management capabilities by finding customers for seats that might otherwise go unfilled.

Both buyers and sellers win, and a new market has emerged around day trading in tickets, hotel accommodations, and anything else that priceline.com imagines buyers and sellers might be willing to trade in this way.

Remember the point we made back in Chapter 2 about how new assets and new markets are being created through New Economy transactions on the Internet? Priceline.com is an example of the highest order.

Asset value grows as the number of transactions increases. Why? Because the interactive informational exchanges between buyers and sellers in this new market make for improved scalability and more efficient matching of supply and demand.

What is the value of this portfolio process to priceline.com? The company's market value at January 1, 2000 was $6.9 billion.

Q: Who is creating value by disposing of organization assets?

A: AT&T Corporation

Perhaps the most dramatic corporate conversion ever (at $101 billion, it was certainly the biggest) occurred in 1996 when AT&T Corporation cut loose two giant pieces of itself. One piece, the former NCR, a computer maker, had been purchased intact by AT&T and was now being returned to independence.

The other piece, of greater interest for our purposes, consisted of the telecommunications equipment manufacturing operation and the famous Bell Laboratories research arm, both of which were brought under the wing of a new company christened Lucent Technologies Inc.

Various explanations were given for AT&T's decision to spin off the Lucent operations. Some observers suggested that AT&T had simply become too big and cumbersome. Robert E. Allen, then AT&T's chief executive officer, told a reporter: "The vertical-integration model was good for its time. But shifts in the market and public policy suggested it was time for us to change."

Among the shifts Allen was referring to: Congress was about to pass the law that allowed AT&T, previously limited to long-distance operations, to compete with regional companies for a piece of the local phone market. It seemed unlikely that the Baby Bells would continue buying switches and other telecommunications equipment from an arm of the company that was fighting with them for customers.

By disposing of assets that were operating below their potential, AT&T has been able to substantially improve its performance and market value. Meanwhile, Lucent has prospered mightily too, and is second only to its former parent as the nation's most widely held stock.

▶ What's next?

Every asset has a life cycle, and certain assets are critical in driving your business model. When you understand the asset life cycle and manage the important processes that drive asset value, new opportunities for creating value emerge.

In the final chapter of this book, we envision a future in which all the assets that matter will finally be measured and reported. Enabled by the next technology revolution, information will open yet another arena of opportunity for companies to create value.

In short, your company needs to understand how to use information to create value, with the goal of ultimately measuring and reporting what matters—both internally and externally. Chapter 13 will show you how to go about it.

Ask Yourself:

- Does your company evaluate its management processes as driving asset value?

- Are you willing to be "disturbed" by the best practices others use to stimulate improvement?

- Does your company have formal processes for managing various types of intangible assets?

- Is your company best-in-class in managing the acquisition, management, renewal, and disposal of your most important assets, both tangible and intangible?

- What changes should your company make to ensure better focus on management of its asset life cycles?

❏

13

Measure and Report All Your Assets.

"The next
information
revolution . . .
largely underlies
the new definition
of the function
of business
enterprise as the
'creation of value
and wealth.'"

—Peter Drucker.[1]

A lot can go wrong in three months. Just ask all those CEOs who have been blindsided by an out-of-the-blue quarterly loss. And ask them what they wouldn't have given for some way to stay on top of their P&L on a daily basis.

Cisco Systems has found the way with a program its CEO, John Chambers, calls the "virtual close." It relies on technology that enables the company to close its financial books on an hour's notice. According to Chambers, 40 percent of those making a pilgrimage to his headquarters in San Jose, California are CFOs and CEOs wanting to know how to do it.

By hooking up an entire company via an intranet and installing the proper applications, Cisco has created an electronic infrastructure that shares all financial data almost instantly. Sales figures, product margins, high-cost structures in a given geographic region—everything is visible in real time. And what that means is a near-miraculous ability to spot problems (and opportunities) as soon as they surface. The potential for strategy enhancements and productivity gains are enormous. A company can truly become proactive rather than reactive. And, needless to say, it can keep a company from being blindsided by a sudden quarterly loss.

Could you benefit from the ability to perform a virtual close? Absolutely. Our main point, however, is that information is at the core of who and what you are as a company. Microsoft's Bill Gates has described such information capabilities "as the corporate, digital equivalent of the human nervous system, providing a well-integrated flow of information to the right part of the organization at the right time . . . [it] is distinguished from a mere network of computers by the accuracy, immediacy, and richness of the information it brings to knowledge workers and the insight and collaboration made possible by the information."[2]

Those who want to compete in this new century will have no choice but to use the power of information in new ways to create value. Why? Because information—the successor to today's measurement and reporting systems—is a crucial part of how companies will create, manage, and measure value in the New Economy. That's the focus of the fourth challenge of value creation in the New Economy. Use information to succeed, measuring and reporting all your assets.

Let's begin with a statement of the problem. Existing information systems fail to reflect the full assets of a business—or the larger economy, for that matter.

To understand the shortcomings of traditional financial statement presentation, just imagine what you would think if your personal investment manager told you, "I'm sorry, but our information systems track only half your assets, and even then, they only tell us what you paid for them." Clearly, that answer would be unacceptable.

How will you and your company cope with this information gap in the future?

! Our prophecy: In the New Economy, companies will need to continuously measure and report all assets at fair value to all users.

How does that prophecy compare to the existing state? Today's measurement and reporting practices can be summed up as follows: Periodic reporting at historic costs with limited disclosures on only a portion of the assets that matter. Our prophecy, simple as it seems, would

Measurement and reporting practices: present and future		Figure 13.1
Measurement/Reporting Framework	Current State	The Future
Reporting framework	Financial statements (preparer and regulator-driven)	Corporate database - electronic library (preparers and users customize reports on an as-needed basis)
Focus	Value realized	Value created (and realized)
What is measured?	Physical and financial assets	All assets - tangible and intangible
Source of information	Internal data	Integrated internal and external data
How measured/reported?	Primarily at historic cost	Fair value. KPIs developed for difficult-to-measure intangible assets
Where delivered?	Hardcopy distribution and limited electronic distribution	Computer desktops and other devices - wherever it is needed
When available?	Periodic	Continuous
In what format?	Number/words	Numbers/words/graphic visualizations and interactive interfaces
To whom reported?	Certain stakeholders as required	All stakeholders eventually
Additional information	Limited	Risk management, strategy, etc.

constitute a revolution: Continuous measurement and reporting all assets to all stakeholders at fair value—when and where that information is needed. Figure 13.1 shows the current state of measurement and reporting in the United States, along side of our vision of what the future holds. Our prophecy would bring change across eight key areas:

What will companies measure?

Where will information come from?

How will companies measure and report performance?

Where will information be delivered?

When will information be available?

In what formats will information be presented?

To whom will companies report?

In what ways will information create value?

Needed changes in information management, measurement, and reporting cannot be achieved overnight, given the challenges of replacing legacy systems, complying with today's regulatory requirements, and developing the tools required for hard-to-measure intangible assets. Nevertheless, companies will need to address all of these questions in the years ahead. The stakes are too high and the rewards too great to sidestep the challenges. Given these realities, we explore what the future may hold across each of the eight questions cited above.

Q: What will you measure?
A: The value of all your assets.

Companies can effectively manage only what they measure. For example, consider how U.S. companies have dealt with health-care benefits for their retirees.

Despite a long tradition of granting benefits for retirees, companies did not historically measure and report these benefits as liabilities. The result: They tended to be generous in granting post-retirement health-care benefits (called OPEB), particularly in exchange for short-term pay concessions from employees.

All that changed in 1991 when the Financial Accounting Standards Board (FASB) ruled that companies had to recognize billions of dollars in health-care liabilities. It was a harsh awakening for many organizations as they discovered the real value of the promises they had made to employees. General Motors Corporation alone had to recognize a $20 billion liability.

A look at the hard numbers quickly convinced most companies to rein in retirement benefits. Those same numbers accelerated the trend toward managed care programs, as companies switched from more costly health insurance offerings to health maintenance organizations (HMOs) or preferred provider plans.

The point here is that no company is immune from the fallout caused by inadequate information for decision-making. Nor should any company wait for regulators to alert it to the need for obtaining information to support value creation. Companies that measured their OPEB obligations properly—even before the FASB acted—were in a position to manage their businesses more effectively.

But how will companies overcome their deficiencies in the area of measuring and reporting all of their assets—tangible and intangible? Every company (yours included) needs to be able to track what is occurring in every asset category among each of its relationships—from construction contracts to customer account management, from recruitment and training to knowledge management, from research and development to investor relations.

Q: Where will information come from?
A: Internal and external sources.

Companies cannot meet this need by focusing only on internal data. They need information about both their own organizations and the external world. As Peter Drucker observed, "All the data we have so far, including those provided by the new tools, focus inward. But inside an enterprise—indeed, even inside the entire economic chain—there are only costs. Results are only on the outside."

To focus your company externally, you need systems that integrate internal data with market information. After all, your company is not an island, nor does it compete in isolation. In fact, it is part of a dynamic market that produces important, two way information flows.

Many of today's technologies—hardware and software—help you to integrate internal data (e.g., enterprise resource planning software). But where do you turn for the ability to combine market data and corporate information?

The right technologies and on-line information portals are quickly emerging. These applications, which will create the next generation of enterprise systems, will make it possible to access external data to benchmark your performance against "the market" in real time. And we don't mean just the customer markets for products and services. Assets are actively traded in many markets, including: Physical (commodities, real estate and other fixed assets); financial (debt and equity); employee and supplier (labor and supply chain); customer (products, services, alliances and channels); and organization (leadership, systems, processes, patents, knowledge, and other intellectual property).

These markets are key sources of assets you need to run your business, and they are becoming more and more efficient by virtue of information flows.

Asset Markets and Market-Makers:
Information Transparencies Emerge

New markets for different kinds of assets have emerged with varying degrees of development and transparency. These markets and the information that drives them are being organized at a rapid pace, as new market-makers and "infomediaries" (many of them now on-line) restructure and improve access to them.

Physical Markets. Information and on-line commerce are dramatically restructuring the commodity markets globally, introducing unprecedented market efficiencies. Witness a service called e-STEEL. Launched in 1999 to provide a "neutral and secure marketplace" for buyers and sellers in the $700 billion global steel industry,[3] e-STEEL, as the market-maker, does not itself own or possess steel products. Rather, the e-STEEL exchange offers a brokering service, bringing buyers and sellers together to initiate and conclude orders on-line.

Employee Markets. The electronic marketplace connecting employees and companies is shaping up to be a low-cost, high-speed, and efficient platform for the labor market. The emerging art of e-cruiting has the potential to eventually displace the $17-billion-a-year U.S. recruiting industry. Even more, the Internet could eliminate newspaper classifieds altogether, according to Forrester Research of Cambridge, Massachusetts. What amounts to the 21st-century version of human auctions is upon us. Monster.com (a popular Internet career site) has launched its Monster Talent Market where job seekers can auction their talent to potential employers, thereby turning the labor market into a true market. Monster.com posts more than 260,000 job opportunities, and on any given day, over 27,000 auctions take place on Monster Talent Market.

Customer Markets. Information makes it easier than ever for your customers to comparison shop. Companies like CompareNet are transforming customer markets by allowing buyers to compare features and prices for everything from toasters to toothbrushes. C2B Technologies is developing powerful search engines that allow consumers to search for products and bargains across the entire Internet. It is also partnering with Consumers' Digest to deliver best-buy recommendations and detailed product reviews. And Third Voice, Inc., offers a free program over the Internet that allows anyone to put electronic "post-it" notes on third-party Web pages. Just imagine: Disillusioned customers will now be able to tell the whole world about their frustrations with your product!

Financial Markets. Nowhere is the transparency and ceaseless flow of information destined to have a greater impact than in the financial markets, which, in turn, will affect your company's relationship with its equity investors. Companies have already figured out that they can access new investors by going outside traditional distribution channels. Indeed, today's technologies and information for decision-making are making global capital markets a reality.

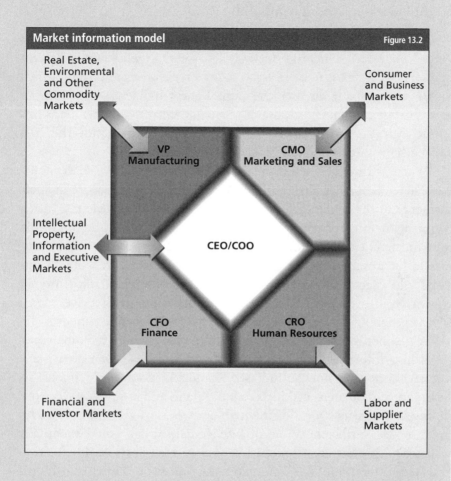

Market information model   Figure 13.2

Real Estate, Environmental and Other Commodity Markets

Consumer and Business Markets

VP Manufacturing

CMO Marketing and Sales

Intellectual Property, Information and Executive Markets

CEO/COO

CFO Finance

CRO Human Resources

Financial and Investor Markets

Labor and Supplier Markets

Organization Markets. New markets are rapidly emerging in the exchange of organization assets. For example, there are several new market-makers targeting transactions in intellectual property. Pl-x.com has established The Patent & License Exchange, Inc., a marketplace for the sale of rated, insured, and independently-priced intellectual property.[4] Intellectual Property Technology Exchange, Inc. has established TechEx, an Internet-based, business-to-business exchange. TechEx links technologies from research laboratories to licensing professionals in life science companies. Patent Auction (www.patentauction.com) provides for purchasing or licensing various forms of intellectual property, including patents, patent applications, technological know-how, trade secrets, copyrights, and trademarks. And BTG plc, a British government research body that was privatized in 1992, has established a transactional Web site (btg-et.com), which offers some 8,500 patents in communication, semi-conductors, integrated media, security and ID, and biomedical.

Q: How will companies measure and report assets?

A: At fair value where available.

A "fair value" standard directly links assets to their value in current markets. This stands in contrast to today's measurement system, which accounts principally for financial capital and tangible assets at historic costs. Companies, in effect, use a "rear-view mirror" to make decisions about their present or future course. Certainly that's not the best approach in a highly dynamic and volatile market.

Where fair market values are not available or cannot be determined, we believe companies must look to innovative ways to measure the performance of their intangible assets. For example, Media Metrix, Inc., a company that describes itself as a pioneer in Internet and digital media measurement, tracks customer assets by such factors as the unique visitors to (or number of "eyeballs browsing") Web sites, Web site "stickiness," Web pages visited, and audience satisfaction indices. The Internet equivalent of television's Nielsen audience measurement service, Media Metrix generates data from more than 50,000 Web-surfing panelists.[5]

A number of companies are already measuring and, in some cases, publishing information about their intangible assets. One of the best known examples is Stockholm-based Skandia Insurance, which markets insurance and financial products to individuals and businesses. Its work in developing a new view of intangible assets started from a powerful premise: Measuring the value of intellectual capital would eventually transform "not just the economy but society itself in its wealth creation and value extraction,"[6] Leif Edvinsson, then-director of intellectual capital, wrote. The company issued its first annual report on intellectual capital in 1995.

The Skandia Intellectual Capital model involves identifying key success factors and performance indicators, which it combines in what the company calls the Skandia Navigator. Many commentators credit the company's focus on its intellectual capital—and the attendant publicity—for much of its growth during the past decade.

Measuring the true drivers of value in your company requires profound examination of what is important to success, not just internally, but to your external stakeholders as well. Note that in our view there is no single set of success factors or key performance indicators (KPIs)

Asset Category	Stock	Flow	Effectiveness
Financial	• Investment value • Cash on hand • Debt-Equity ratio	• Free cash flow • Days of receivables	• Return on investment • Cash flow per employee
Physical	• Inventory on hand • Fixed asset investment • Square feet office space	• Inventory turnover • Depreciation • Growth in office space	• Inventory carrying cost • Return on assets; machine utilization • Occupancy
Customer	• Number of customers • Market share	• Customer churn	• Customer satisfaction • Revenue per customer
Employee & Supplier	• Number of employees • Number of suppliers	• Employee turnover/ retention • Number of suppliers meeting strategic criteria	• Revenue per employee • Procurement costs • Ability to recruit employees and change suppliers • Employee understanding of strategy
Organization	• Number of patents	• R & D expenditures • Succession plan	• Licensing income as % of R&D • Successful business strategy • Revenue from products < 3 years

Example stock, flow and effectiveness KPIs — Figure 13.3

that make sense for every business. Take AT&T and Home Depot, for instance. AT&T might focus on customer retention as a KPI because of the unique competitive environment of the long-distance communications industry. In contrast, Home Depot might focus more on "revenue per customer visit" to monitor in-store sales and the overall shopping experience.

To illustrate, we have developed examples of KPIs across the five Value Dynamics asset classes. They are based on three types of measures: stock, that is, some statement of the quantity or value of an asset; flows, referring to the life cycle and rate of change of the asset; and effectiveness, addressing the efficiency with which specific outcomes are achieved. It is a combination of existing and emerging measures, including KPIs, that will allow companies, including yours, to measure tangible and intangible assets at fair value.

Q: Where will information be delivered?

A: At the corporate desktop and wherever else it is needed.

The New Economy has already shown us that information can be integrated and delivered everywhere people need it, on devices previously unimagined. That includes both at work and home, on computer desktops and laptops, via your personal digital assistants (PDAs), and other digital devices, including wireless phones and pagers.

But "where" information is delivered is only half the equation. Knowledge in the New Economy is increasingly customized to individual needs. That trend has been well established by my.yahoo! and portfolio management tools offered by numerous on-line financial service companies, including E*TRADE and Schwab.

For business users, however, that same concept of customized information available ubiquitously is yet to be fully realized. Information customized to your needs, for example, might mean market-based data

> **Who will be the first to create a "Bloomberg" for business? Is there an emerging Yahoo! look-alike to deliver personalized business information?**

on all of your key assets, combined with continuous updates of the company's revenues and expenses.

Businesses, like consumers and investors, are unique and live in real-time. Who will be the first to create a "Bloomberg" for business as a whole? What information company will step forward to build an AOL for corporate America—"Business Online" (BOL) perhaps? Is there an emerging Yahoo! look-alike that will offer customized and individualized business information?

Some managers may question whether their company really needs such a robust and ubiquitous information capability. Our answer: Yes. In fact, we are convinced that companies in years to come will have many choices of providers that will organize real-time market data feeds for everyone's desktop or other locations.

Who will build these systems? As we write this, systems dubbed

Enterprise Information Portals (EIPs) are becoming a reality.[7]   To quote a study by Merrill Lynch, an EIP will enable "companies to unlock internally and externally stored information, and provide users [with] a single gateway to customized information needed to make informed business decisions."

When will this be a reality? Sooner than you think, as enterprise software providers like SAP, Oracle, and PeopleSoft respond to the challenge of the Internet and new business-to-business success stories (Ariba, Inc., for example, which sells supply chain software) and seek to connect their existing customers to the world around them.

Q: When will information be made available?
A: Continuously, 24 x 7.

Our view is that continuous measurement and reporting will become the "gold-standard" for companies. Again, this is in sharp contrast to the periodic reporting practices that prevail today.

Businesses operate 24 hours a day, 7 days a week across multiple time zones. Yet information generated by companies often reflects monthly, quarterly, or annual milestones. Although our envisaged 24 x 7 measurement and reporting model deals primarily with the frequency of reporting, it also speaks to the crucial need for information relevant to managing a global business in the New Economy. Witness Cisco's virtual close, which was described earlier. We believe it is a harbinger of the future.

But Cisco, as we noted, does not stand alone. Steven M.H. Wallman, a former Securities and Exchange (SEC) Commissioner, is an ardent supporter of new "user-customized" systems in which investors and other interested parties have direct access to a broad set of corporate data (financial and nonfinancial). He believes that real-time reporting systems will ultimately spell the demise of periodic reporting. These systems will offer direct access to data about key value drivers, data that can be aggregated and disaggregated by the users as desired and for their individual purposes.

"Businesses are run on a continuous basis, not a quarterly basis," he recently told an audience. Without "the artificiality of the quarterly reporting system," activities "like trying to move inventory at the end of a certain quarter in order to show an uptick in revenues" would disappear.

"Analysts and investors," Wallman went on, "would judge a stock based on a company's performance and prospects, not on how well it manages to a certain number four times a year."[8]

How will this occur? Once again, we look to the financial markets to see the future. Here, real-time information and analytics are the de facto standard. Why shouldn't your company demand the same types of capabilities? And why shouldn't all corporate stakeholders—including investors, employees, and customers—benefit? Our answer: They should.

As we noted earlier, emerging technologies will set the pace as they allow forward-thinking companies to derive information daily or even hourly through information delivered to the corporate desktop. Technology capabilities (e.g., the Enterprise Information Portals described above) will alter what your company can measure and report—and the way it sources information—both internally and externally.

Q: In what formats will information be presented?
A: Numeric, text, and graphic visualization.

As Paul Saffo, director and Roy Amara Fellow of the Institute for the Future, once described it, we are "afloat in a growing sea of information." He believes the most important tools of the next decade will be those that help people "visualize and simulate . . . to reduce vast and obscure pools of data into easily comprehended images."

Information will be organized in ways that allow management, employees, and investors to visualize asset performance; data will be analyzed to reveal investment patterns and their impact on value. New forms of graphic visualization will join the traditional presentations of information in numbers and text.

But how far can today's emerging visual capabilities go? A long way. In fact, your local weather channel already offers a view of what is possible in the corporate world. Weather reports use key data in three areas—temperature, pressure, and humidity. Behind these representations lie complex computations and simulations that often require supercomputers. Nevertheless, they can be displayed in simple, visual formats.[9]

Similar capabilities using visualization already exist for handling health care and engineering information. It is only a matter of time before the new formats arrive in business.

Q: To whom will companies report?

A: All stakeholders.

The revolution in measuring and reporting what matters cannot stop at the company's front door. Why? Because no organization or its leadership creates value in isolation, particularly not when sources of value and capital include so many external shareholders. Because a company is an extended enterprise, questions about information disclosure apply to the company's value chain of relationships—customers, employees, suppliers, partners, and investors.

Moreover, we think the premium for openness (or transparency) is going to rise dramatically in the coming years. Research shows that

> Technology itself becomes a pressure,
> as well as an enabler, for wider reporting.

reporting more to investors and other stakeholders than is required under law can benefit an organization. We are already seeing investors, customers, employees, and other partners flocking to those companies that are providing the best information for informed decision-making. Companies that gain a reputation for openness are likely to find a market more forgiving of occasional bad news. Investors will reward such openness by reducing the rate of return they require from a company, thereby lowering the company's cost of capital.

Technology itself becomes a pressure, as well as an enabler, for wider reporting. In a speech before The Brookings Institution, Wallman noted that the "power of the Internet and technological changes generally will be an irresistible force—a positive force—in financial reporting in the future." That's because users of financial information are more diverse, as are their needs. And they are demanding more meaningful, detailed and disaggregated information, rather than one-size-fits-all reports.

And, Wallman added, the standard financial disclosures available are "now just starting to work towards disclosure models that address the kinds of assets that are increasingly driving the market capitalization of public companies—intellectual and human capital and knowledge assets such as intellectual property."[10]

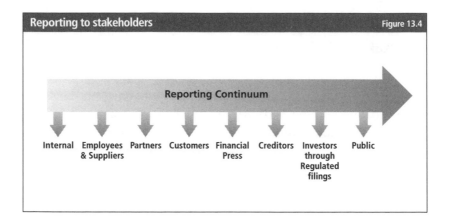

Reporting to stakeholders   Figure 13.4

Reporting Continuum

Internal   Employees   Partners   Customers   Financial   Creditors   Investors   Public
           & Suppliers   Press   through
                                                                       Regulated
                                                                       filings

How will this affect you? The realities of today's regulatory environment for financial reporting, of course, will remain a critical shaper of practices. Even now, many nations and companies are importing and endorsing the highly-regulated approach that has evolved in the United States. In addition, pressures to harmonize accounting, auditing and governance standards around the globe are forcing countries in this direction. But the technological capacity to move and access large amounts of information in many formats provides a significant counter-force to the influence of standardized financial statements.

Against this backdrop of increasing information availability and dissemination, we believe an incremental approach to external financial reporting makes sense. Your company needs to experiment with fair value reporting—beginning first with internal reports, then expanding gradually to include other stakeholders.

In Figure 13.4, note the information flow beginning on the left, a company's internal reporting for management decision-making. The next step along the continuum includes information released to employees and suppliers, partners and customers. We also include the financial press. In the United States, for example, certain types of high-level financial and non-financial information that has relevance to financial statements are disclosed to the press and analysts periodically (e.g., appointment of key managers, holiday sales highlights). These releases typically precede the issuance of audited financial statements that investors receive. At the far right in the continuum we include the public (e.g., community), of which a company is a part. When Internet-based, continuous reporting becomes a reality, these gaps in timing will vanish as interested parties have access to information on demand, most likely through links to a company's Web site.

While an "incremental" approach has merit, however, there's no reason to delay action. In the long run, the reporting framework itself must change. What is needed is an information revolution—and in the New Economy, the leaders of that revolution will determine not only their own future, but yours as well.

Q: In what ways will information create value?
A: Every company is an information company at heart.

As the millennium ended, General Motors Corporation and Ford Motor Company demonstrated that every company is an information company with potential to create value in this realm. These rival giants each announced plans to launch eBusiness Internet sites—global electronic forums for all the goods and services they buy. "By the end of 2001, we're going to expect all of General Motors' purchases to go through this site, and we would expect all of our suppliers to be as actively engaged," said Harold Kutner, head of purchasing for General Motors.[11] The sites are expected to have major impact.

The top two U.S. automakers are hoping they can save billions of dollars by replacing networks of personal contacts and paper forms with an electronic capability that allows for almost instant transactions. Both companies report they want suppliers to use the eBusiness Web sites to make purchases or sell excess inventory. General Motors describes GM TradeXchange as a "virtual Internet community" that should help suppliers by streamlining purchases and promoting lower costs. GM launched the site in late 1999.

General Motors has more than 30,000 suppliers, with the automaker spending about $87 billion annually. Mr. Kutner has estimated that General Motors' site could be handling sales near $500 billion in a few years.[12] Market researcher Dataquest estimates that these massive sites could help propel eBusiness from approximately $200 billion a year to at least $1 trillion annually in the next two or three years.

Remember Lou Gerstner's prediction, which we noted in Chapter 10? Many of the eBusiness companies of the 1990s will be but "fireflies before the storm" when compared to what will occur when the giant companies and institutions seize the power of the global information infrastructure.

As we have seen, improved information—supported by changes in the measurement and reporting system as a whole—will benefit your organization in numerous ways. It will allow management to identify

The GM and Ford sites could help propel eBusiness from about $200 billion a year to at least $1 trillion annually in the next two to three years.

business opportunities and threats continuously. Put another way, it sets a stage for businesses to master risk. By communicating relevant and timely information to market participants, companies will increase investor confidence, thereby lowering the cost of capital. Improved information and reporting also supports strategic decision-making, which can make you a "first mover" in your markets.

Clearly, it makes sense to start now to transform your own information, measurement, and reporting systems. And to help you begin, we have developed the Value Dynamics Information Framework (Figure 13.5). It responds to many of the concerns we've just addressed.

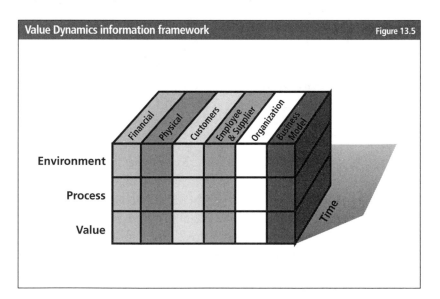

Value Dynamics information framework   Figure 13.5

The Value Dynamics Information Framework integrates internal and external information about markets. It sets an agenda for collecting information across the entire asset base of a company. It helps an organization answer key questions. What information do you have about the extended environment and your company's processes and value? How do you track this information over time?

The goal: A company-wide information system that takes advantage of the transparency of information in the New Economy and tracks all of the assets that matter. Information networked in this way will become the lifeblood of your future, making possible decision-making that enhances corporate value and manages business risk.

Building this system will transform your company into an enterprise with information at its core. But, as we all know, the corporation doesn't stand alone, particularly in a regulated environment. Regulatory units and other public bodies will continue to have great influence over measurement and reporting. Consider what will be needed to make our prophecy about measurement and reporting a reality.

▶ Call to Action

We end this chapter, and our book, with a call to action, urging all stakeholders to use information to create value in the New Economy. What will that require in the years ahead? Concerted efforts by all.

- Management must strive to obtain complete, real-time information about the fair value of all their assets so that they can set strategy, master risk, and measure and report on the entire value creation process.

- Boards of directors need information about all the assets that drive value so that they can properly discharge their duties of stewardship and governance.

- Investors should demand information transparency so that they direct resources where they will create the most value.

- Employees should actively participate in open, two-way communication with employers to enhance their ability to create value for themselves and others.

- Customers should seek out organizations that understand and address their needs so that they and their suppliers will prosper.

- Standard-setters and regulators should encourage the development of new measurement and reporting systems that enhance information transparency.

- And, finally, policy-makers should promote the measurement and reporting of all sources of value to all stakeholders so that they have a sound basis for developing monetary, fiscal and social policies.

▶ What's next?

As we have seen, change is inevitable. The New Economy is signaling a massive shift in value creation for both business and society. How will these issues transform our world in the years ahead? That is the subject of the Epilogue.

Ask Yourself:

- What are your company's principal sources of information? Are these sources primarily internal or external?

- Does your company collect information on all the assets that create value in the New Economy?

- How does your company gather information about its markets? Does it maintain electronic links to various data and information sources?

- Are there systems in place at your company to integrate internal information with external information about the marketplace?

- Do you regularly communicate with all your stakeholders about your company's long-term sources of value?

EPILOGUE
Leave a Legacy of Value.

"To my mind,
there must be,
at the bottom
of it all,
not an equation,
but an utterly
simple idea."

—John Archibald Wheeler

F orget the hype of Internet day traders. Forget the hysteria of Dow 12,000 or 15,000 or 30,000, and the 5,000 NASDAQ. The daily ups and downs of the markets, so breathlessly reported by the media, are not what the New Economy is about. Through the static, the signal sounds clear: There is lasting new found value being created. In the final analysis, that is the ultimate reward of this new millennium, whether bull market or bear.

To be sure, the New Economy owes a debt to the auspicious coming-together of new technologies and communications, eBusiness and the Internet, work-life issues, and changes in public policy.

But at its core is the economic and social power of intangibles—relationships, knowledge, and intellectual property—multiplied by the effects of the networked global economy. Years from now, when the books are written about what drove all this value, the answer will be the one we suggested in these pages—the relationships a company has with all its stakeholders (investors, employees, suppliers and customers), and the knowledge derived from them.

Today, government policy, business strategy, risk management, process improvement, and reporting are still primarily shaped by the industrial economy and the centuries-old measurement system that preceded it. But business leaders, regulators, politicians and academics alike are struggling to find a new language and a new set of principles to describe the New Economy revolution, to understand the underpinnings of success in this new age, and to reinvent the legacy of measurement.

One noted example and exemplar of that effort, who needs little introduction, is Warren E. Buffett, the chairman of Berkshire Hathaway Inc. In his occasional public appearances and his wise and witty annual reports, Buffett talks of his concept of intrinsic value, which he defines as "the discounted value of the cash that can be taken out of a business during its remaining life." It is his effort to establish a value for a company that moves beyond the narrow limits of book value, as arrived at by traditional accounting systems.

In his User's Manual for stockholders, he draws the distinction between intrinsic and book value using a college education as his text. The cost of the schooling, he says, is its book value. The intrinsic economic value of the education is represented by the extra earnings the student will receive because of her degree, minus the income she would have generated

As Warren Buffett says: "Book value is meaningless as an indicator of intrinsic value."

had she gone to work instead of school for four years. If the graduate flunks out, book value may end up exceeding intrinsic value; otherwise, intrinsic value is going to be far greater. Either way, Buffett says, "Book value is meaningless as an indicator of intrinsic value."

What Warren Buffett is suggesting is a kind of economic heresy today. But it is sure to become the new canon tomorrow. Imagine that in the not-so-distant future, it has become clear that what is most enduring is also what is most intangible—relationships and knowledge. At the same time, what was once regarded and measured as an asset (for example, things) is now regarded as an expense. In other words, these are costs to be eschewed, areas to be cut—whenever and wherever possible.

On the other hand, everything that was either defined as an expense or overlooked (people, customers, research and development, insight) is now an asset—something to be acquired and cherished.

Such a scenario would have extraordinary implications for some of the companies profiled in this book—not to mention its impact on your own enterprise and the world economy.

For example, Toys "R" Us and Wal-Mart have been phenomenally successful retailers. Both companies built storefront after storefront around the globe. But in our hypothetical future world, the balance sheets of these companies would be significantly smaller because they would have expensed all of their investments in brick and mortar.

In this future world, New Economy competitor eBay.com, an Internet auctioneer with a market capitalization rivaling or exceeding that of its old-world rivals, has capitalized its entire base of customers and supply-chain assets. Its balance sheet has exploded in value as it has continued to invest in intangibles.

But there's more to see in our through-the-looking-glass world of the future. Real estate companies are now expensing their entire asset bases each month, reducing once-hefty balance sheets. In contrast, America Online and other Internet companies are sporting extraordinary value comprised of capitalized customer and knowledge assets.

And what does the future hold for the world of international trade? When software code is shipped between nations, it appears in their trade accounts at fair market value, equal to or surpassing the value of transactions involving physical assets like raw materials or cars, altering forever the calculations underlying the balance of trade.

In the decades ahead, as we envision them, values are the polar opposite of what people were accustomed to in pre-millennial times. A

> ## In this futuristic scenario, values are the polar opposite of what we are accustomed to today.

more contemporary view of wealth and well-being has emerged.

But let's take our thesis a bit further. As this book went to press, 90 percent of the human genetic code had been mapped. And with the mapping scheduled to be completed in the next few years, the entire genetic map for humans will become a reality—an accomplishment that will transform forever the health care industry, as we know it. New drugs and treatments will become a reality. Armed with this map of the genetic code, health care professionals will be able to diagnose diseases before symptoms appear and prescribe individually tailored designer drugs to fit each unique genetic make-up. This reality is now within reach.

Of course, this is not a health care book, and we are still some distance from fully breaking the code of business value. However, let's compare the path in cracking the value code in business to Francis Crick's and James Watson's research into the basic structure of DNA some 40 years ago. Our first step has been to identify the five basic

The challenge: to develop new systems of information, measurement and reporting that properly identify what creates value.

building blocks of value in business—physical, financial, employee and supplier, customer, and organization assets. This step was essential before going further in mapping the code of value creation.

Insight into how the basic components of value are shared by every enterprise is another step in the right direction. So is understanding that the unique combinations and proportions of these assets make up a company's business model and determine its economic value more directly than industry. This has important implications for corporate leadership. With different types and combinations of assets creating value, new leadership styles and capabilities must follow.

With this knowledge, we have argued that the revolutionary changes driving business success today demand a global effort to understand the value of the assets that count in the New Economy.

The Value Dynamics Framework is a beginning. We hope that our research and insights into what creates value, the tools to visualize it, and the processes to enhance and sustain it, will inspire you to look at your company's portfolio of assets and its value code in a new light. We hope it will help you see, invest in and manage the assets that count most in the New Economy. We hope it will help you create a greater store of corporate wealth and personal worth in the years ahead.

In this book, we have offered a comprehensive analysis of value derived from the marketplace. Our model, as described above, also has relevance for governments and not-for-profit organizations. The principles of Value Dynamics can guide public policy makers to produce economic environments that promote value creation.

But much remains to be done in developing new systems of management, measurement, and reporting, to properly define what does and does not create value for business and society, for both the public and the private sectors. We invite you to take part in our on-line forum dedicated to exploring how companies create, manage, and measure value creation in the New Economy. Visit us at www.arthurandersen.com/value.

Our exploration together constitutes a noble purpose for this generation of business and political leaders and holds out the possibility of providing a lasting legacy for generations to come.

GLOSSARY

Certain words and phrases used to describe Value Dynamics and the New Economy have taken on new meaning. Some of the distinctions are subtle, others involve wholesale change. In many cases, our definitions differ from strict accounting definitions. To prevent misunderstanding, we set out a glossary of pertinent terms as they are used in this book.

Affiliates. In Value Dynamics terminology, affiliates are part of the customer asset category. The purpose of these inter-organizational relationships is to facilitate the marketing and sales of products and services. They are an example of networking and connectivity.

Assets. Value Dynamics defines assets as all potential sources of future economic benefit that have the capacity to contribute to a company's overall value. Assets are tangible and intangible. They are not limited by concepts of ownership or control; for example, assets include relationships, which are not subject to contractual ties. Assets are the core building blocks of value, even though many important assets (e.g., customer relationships, channel assets, reputation) don't currently show up on a company's balance sheet.

Asset life cycle. An asset's value-creating life, which includes acquisition, deployment, retention and renewal, and disposition. A warehouse, for instance, may be built or bought, put to use for housing inventory, renovated to accommodate new products or technology, and eventually torn down to make way for something else. Intangible assets also have a life cycle. For example, the effectiveness of a business strategy in creating value will decline over time as markets evolve until it eventually becomes obsolete.

Brand. This organization asset embodies more than just the image conveyed by a product's name, trademarks, credentials, expertise, packaging, etc. In the New Economy, brands represent your company's reputation, based on the interactions of your employees, and products and services, with customers, suppliers, and other stakeholders. They are the external manifestation of your strategy and culture.

Buildings. These assets are tangible structures that, in most cases, are permanently anchored to the ground below and are fit for human habitation. This physical asset includes factories, offices, and warehouses, no matter how they're designed or what they're made of, because proper management can turn these fixed assets into a solid house of value creation.

Business model. The unique combination of tangible and intangible assets that drives an organization's ability to create or destroy value.

Cash. Currency on hand and demand deposits held in financial institutions are included in the financial asset category. So are highly liquid short-term investments (or cash equivalents) such as money market funds and U.S. Treasury bills. Free cash flow is the amount left over after providing working capital to the company's businesses, making investments, and paying dividends and interest.

Channels. Channel assets are a critical link in the flow of merchandise or services from a supplier to the consumer or end-user. Channel assets — wholesale and retail companies, for example—are an integral part of any company's go-to-market model. They fall into the customer asset category. In the New Economy, channels like the Internet open the door to bigger audiences and markets than ever before and make scalability possible.

Culture and Values. Culture represents a company's style or personality formed over time by its collective relationships. Values are an element of a company's "core ideology," that is the enduring character of an organization. (See James C. Collins and Jerry I. Porras, "Building Your Company's Vision," *Harvard Business Review*, September-October 1996). Values are defined as guiding principles, or minimum, non-negotiable standards of behavior.

Customers. These buyers of a product or service are a primary source of value to any organization. They are one of the assets in the customer asset category.

Customer Assets. An intangible asset category that includes not only the end-users of a product or service, but also a company's channels and affiliates. Each is an essential link in the outbound value chain that runs from the origination of goods and services to the ultimate consumers.

Debt. In traditional accounting terms, debt is simply a liability. Value Dynamics, however, includes a company's ability to raise debt as a value-creating asset within the financial asset category. A company usually takes on debt—money owed to an outside party—by floating a bond offering or arranging for a term loan.

Employees. Sometimes referred to as human capital, this asset in the employee and supplier asset category includes everyone at every level of an organization who works for financial and other compensation (e.g., salary, stock options, bonuses, organizational position and status perquisites). The value of employees lies in their skills, knowledge, experience, attitudes, and commitment. It is enhanced by an organization's ability to hire, train, motivate, and retain the best people.

Employee and Supplier Assets. This category of intangible assets consists of an organization's employees, members of its inbound supply chain, and its partners. All bring or supply skills, knowledge, connections, or products and services.

Equipment. Any tool or piece of machinery, from a popcorn popper to a printing press, that is used to carry out a particular business task. This physical asset includes computers and other tangible products of the digital age.

Equity. Value Dynamics includes equity as a financial asset because the ability to raise equity by issuing stock spreads risk over many investors and generates a form of currency that can be used to create greater value. Equity represents an ownership interest in the residual assets of an entity after liabilities are deducted.

Financial Assets. These assets include cash, receivables, investments, and sources of debt and equity. These days, almost anything, from home mortgages to David Bowie's future royalties from old recordings, can be converted into financial assets in the form of marketable securities. A financial asset holds its place in the Value Dynamics framework so long as it is a source of capital that can be exploited to create value.

Inventory. Finished goods, partly finished goods, and work in process are held for sale in the ordinary course of business. Raw materials consumed in the production process are also part of the physical asset category, as are supplies used in a company's everyday operations.

Investments. The common stocks, bonds, and other financial securities and instruments bought by both individual and corporate investors are part of the financial asset category. A company generally makes minority investments in the securities of another company or joint venture in the hope of increasing its overall market value.

Land. Land is a piece of real estate, including improvements, that a company holds for productive use or investment. Land falls in the physical asset category.

Leadership. The capacity to inspire, organize, direct, and manage the value-creation process is categorized as an organization asset in the Value Dynamics Framework.

New Economy. The new economic environment which emerged in the late 1990s, is the result of numerous convergent forces: new communications and Internet technologies, globalization, industry consolidation, a new generation of people entering the workplace, and the increased importance of intangible assets such as knowledge, relationships, and intellectual property. In the New Economy, companies are using previously unrecognized assets to create unprecedented value.

Organization Assets. These intangible assets provide the glue supporting an organization's ability to compete, and enable it to respond in a coherent way to the challenges of the New Economy. They include leadership, strategy, structure, values, brand, innovation, knowledge, systems, processes and intellecutal property. Organization assets enable one asset to work with another, one system to talk to another, and one decision to mesh with another.

Partners. Part of the category of employee and supplier assets, partners are defined as parties that come together as joint principals in a business venture (meaning a contractual arrangement in which two or more partners exercise joint control). Partners may also include alliance partners and affiliates.

Physical Assets. Land, buildings, equipment, and inventory—the things you can see and touch, count and weigh—make up this category of tangible assets. They are central to strategic decisions about a company's real estate investments, its productive capacity, the security of its raw materials supply, and its finished goods inventory.

Processes. The series of operations, methods, actions, tasks, or functions leading to the creation of an end-product or service. Processes, which are part of the organization asset category, encompass the day-to-day business operations of a company and how it manages each and every asset.

Proprietary Knowledge. This asset can be defined as concepts, ideas, inventions, literary creations, software programs, or any other creative work that is definable, measurable, and exclusive to a particular company. Proprietary knowledge is included in the organization asset grouping.

Receivables. These are claims a business expects to collect from customers and others who have bought goods or services or otherwise promised to pay a certain sum of money at a specified time. Receivables, part of the financial asset category, are listed on a company's balance sheet.

Risk. Risk represents the uncertainty of future reward—both in terms of the upside and downside. The New Economy brings increased risk as old business models become obsolete and new business models offer unprecedented opportunities. Risk and opportunity are two sides of the same coin.

Scalability. Companies can create value by scaling assets—e.g., using new technologies to exponentially expand the reach and usefulness of assets and business models. If the business environment changes (e.g., customer tastes and preferences alter), scalability also refers to the ability to curtail the scale of operations appropriately.

Strategy. Within the Value Dynamics context, corporate strategy concerns the effective design and execution of a business model to create and realize value. Value Dynamics also gives examples of specific asset portfolio strategies. These include build, enhance, convert, connect and block strategies to enhance asset portfolio values.

Structure. The hierarchy of an organization, often represented by an organization chart, defines how the organization works. Structure is an asset in the organization asset category.

Suppliers. Members of the inbound supply chain who furnish materials, products, or services to an organization. The chain extends to a company's primary suppliers, the suppliers' suppliers, and so on down the line.

Systems. The evolving rules and protocols that management deploys, principally in electronic form, to gather and organize information to support and link business processes and to ensure that the different components of an organization interact efficiently. Systems are part of the organization asset category.

Value. In financial terms, the value of an asset to an individual is the cash amount at which the individual is prepared to buy or sell the asset. The market value of an asset is the amount at which buyers and sellers actually agree to buy and sell. Fair value is the amount for which an asset could be exchanged between knowledgeable and willing parties in an arm's length transaction. This will generally equate to market value where market information is available. The market capitalization of a quoted company is represented by the total market value of its equity shares.

Value Creation. Value creation is the increase in value derived from investments in a portfolio of tangible and intangible assets. Increases in stock market prices reflect market estimates of value creation in the period as embodied in changes in estimated future cash flows, often projected years or even decades into the future.

Value Dynamics. An asset-centric and integrated approach to business strategy in the New Economy. Value Dynamics suggests that the combinations and proportions of assets constituting or representing the business model determine economic outcomes. Value Dynamics provides a holistic approach to meeting four challenges of value creation in the New Economy: designing a business model, mastering risk, managing the asset portfolio, and measuring and reporting the organization's entire asset base.

Value Dynamics Framework. This framework classifies assets into five broad categories—physical, financial, employee and supplier, customer, and organization. The framework thus provides a way to identify and organize all of a company's sources of value creation. It expands the existing accounting framework to include both tangible and intangible assets, as well as sources of value inside the organization and external to it.

Value Imaging. A user-friendly, visual approach to graphic presentation of the Value Dynamics Framework. Value Imaging uses a graphical user interface to depict a company's business model in terms of value contributed by each of the five asset categories. It can also be used to depict other variables, including investment in or divestment of assets, and the associated risks.

Value Realization. Value is realized in the form of earnings or cash flows. Value realization is at the heart of the current accounting and financial reporting frameworks, and therefore focuses primarily on current or historical performance.

SOURCES & SUGGESTED READING

Introduction

1 C.K. Scott-Moncrieff and Terence Kilmartin (translators), *Remembrance of Things Past* (New York: Random House, 1982).
2 David Wessel. "From Greenspan, a (Truly) Weighty Idea," *Wall Street Journal*, May 20, 1999, p. B1.
3 Editors, "Handbook of the Business Revolution - Manifesto," *Fast Company*, November 1995, p. 8.
4 Thomas Petzinger, Jr., *The New Pioneers—The Men and Women Who Are Transforming the Workplace and Marketplace* (New York: Simon & Schuster), p. 5.

Chapter One

1 Sources of information on America Online, Inc. include: Catherine Yang, Peter Burrows, Michael Moeller, "The 800-Pound Gorilla of E-Commerce," *Business Week*, April 5, 1999, p. 100; Marc Gunther, Liz Smith, Wilton Woods, "The Internet is Mr. Case's Neighborhood," *Fortune*, March 30, 1998, p. 68; "Making AOL A-O.K.," *Business Week*, January 11, 1999, p. 65; Kelley Holland (Editor), "A New Doorway at AOL," *Business Week*, August 3, 1998, p. 42; 1998 Annual Report; Steve Case, "Chairman's Letter;" www.aol.com; www.hoovers.com; Compustat through FAME's Information Service; SmartMoney; and Microsoft's MoneyCentral.
2 Sources of information on Time Warner, Inc. include: Compustat through FAME's Information Service; SmartMoney; and Microsoft's MoneyCentral.
3 In the key data performance charts shown for companies throughout the book, the key data is sourced from Compustat through FAME's Information Service, SmartMoney, and www.hoovers.com. Each graph plots market capitalization on the company's financial quarter-ending date (data sourced from Compustat and FAME's US Pricing Database). However, the Q4 1999 data on market value is latest shares outstanding on January 7, 2000 (sourced from SmartMoney) multiplied by the closing price on December 31, 1999 (sourced from FAME's US Pricing Database).
   The graph also plots the index of the average change in market value of the appropriate industry sector (source, SmartMoney). The index is set to the value of the organization at the beginning of the period.
   Terms are defined as follows:
   - Market Cap—The market value of the organization is calculated by multiplying the stock price by the number of shares outstanding. The one-year growth is the difference between the market cap of the date shown and the market cap of one year earlier, as a percentage of the market cap of the year earlier.
   - Book Value—The book value is shareholder equity, which is calculated by subtracting total liabilities from total assets, both of which are selected from the balance sheet.
   - % of market cap is the book value as a percentage of market cap on that same date.
   - Sales—is selected from the income statement or P&L for the 12 months
   - Net income—is selected from the income statement or P&L for the 12 months
   - Employees—is the number of employees at the date shown
   - Price Earnings ratio—is the share price divided by shareholder earnings
   - Volatility—is the one year historic volatility of the stock price
4 Sources for material on Dell Computer Corporation include: Michael Dell, "Power of Virtual Integration," *Harvard Business Review*, March-April 1998, p. 72; Michael S. Dell, "Chairman's Letter," Dell Corporation, 1997 Annual Report; Michael S. Dell, "Chairman's Letter," 1998 Annual Report; Michael S. Dell and Catherine Fredman, *Direct From Dell* (HarperBusiness, 1999); Richard Murphy, "Michael Dell," *Success*, January 1999, p. 50; David Kline, "Discovering New

251

Value in Intellectual Property," *Harvard Business Review,* January-February, 2000; Andrew E. Serwer, "Michael Dell Turns the PC World Inside Out," *Fortune,* September 8, 1997, p. 76; Bernard Wysocki, Jr., "Corporate Caveat: Dell or be Delled," *Wall Street Journal,* May 10, 1999, p. A1; www.Dell.com; Compustat through FAME's Information Service; SmartMoney; and Microsoft's MoneyCentral.

5 *Fortune,* September 6, 1999.

6 Sources for material on Gap Inc. include: Melanie Kletter and Thomas Cunningham, "Gap Net Up 45.6 Percent, Penney's Rises 3 Percent," *WWD,* February 26, 1999, p. 2; Nina Munk, "Gap Gets It," *Fortune,* August 3, 1998, p. 68; "Daddy Gap," *Business Week,* January 11, 1999, p. 63; The Gap, Inc., 1997 Annual Report; www.gap.com; Compustat through FAME's Information Service; SmartMoney; and Microsoft's MoneyCentral.

7 Dow Jones Industry Groups, *Wall Street Journal,* January 3, 2000, page R39.

8 The market value of a business is computed mathematically as the number of shares outstanding multiplied by the stock price. The book value of a business is an aggregation of its financial assets and liabilities at their mostly historical amounts together with historical costs and revenues carried forward to future periods.

9 For example, in 1997, Daniel Collins, Edward Maydew, and Ira Weiss found that, contrary to claims in professional literature, the combined value-relevance of earnings and book values have remained strong and have not declined over the past 40 years (1953 to 1993). See Daniel Collins, Edward L. Maydew, and Ira S. Weiss, "Changes in the Value-Relevance of Earnings and Book Values Over the Past Forty Years," *Journal of Accounting & Economics,* volume. 24, pp. 39-67. This result is consistent with the general conclusions of Jennifer Francis and Katherine Schipper and K. Ely and Gregory Waymire who find no consistent evidence that value-relevance has declined over time. See K. Ely and Gregory Waymire, "Accounting Standard-Setting Organizations and Earnings Relevance," working paper, 1996, Emory University, Atlanta, Georgia. See also Jennifer Francis and Katherine Schipper, "Have Financial Statements Lost Their Relevance?" working paper, 1996, University of Chicago, Chicago, Illinois. In contrast, however, J. Chang concluded, based on a variety of methodologies, that the value relevance of earnings and book value has decreased over the past 40 years. See J. Chang, "The Decline in Value Relevance of Earnings and Book Values," 1998, working paper, Harvard University.

10 "New Math for a New Economy," *Fast Company,* December 14, 1999, www.fastcompany.com/on-line.

11 The research consisted of charting analyses using a database comprised of all active publicly traded companies in the United States. This includes approximately 10,000 active and inactive companies that are traded in the New York Stock Exchange, the American Stock Exchange, and the NASDAQ. The database included information on approximately 450 publicly reported facts per company from 1978 to 1996 at an annual frequency filed with the Securities & Exchange Commission (SEC), as reported by Compustat. Total shareholder returns over one- and five-year periods were calculated using the FAME North American Equities database.

12 The analysis used the Compustat database of approximately 10,000 U.S. public companies. A goal of the research was to look at value creation independent of company size, revenues, earnings or other current financial measures. To avoid analyzing only large companies, our researchers employed the ratio of market value to net sales. We also excluded companies of very small size since they had yet to mature as value-creators. The total database after these adjustments included 3,500 public companies. Organizations were sorted based on market value divided by net sales, and then divided into 10 groups (deciles) and five groups (quintiles). Meaningful results were found using both deciles and quintiles; even the smallest group (a decile group of 350 companies) was large enough to be statistically sound. The eleven Standard & Poor's industry categories were used to group industries.

13 Arthur Andersen teamed with DYG, Inc. and the Health Forum (a wholly owned subsidiary of the American Hospital Association) in 1998 to conduct a survey of senior executives on issues relating to value creation. Survey research was conducted by DYG, Inc.

14 Sources of material on Microsoft Corporation include: George Tibbits, "Microsoft worth a half-trillion dollars", *The Austin American-Statesman,* July 19, 1999, p. D11; Nikhil Deogun and Kara Scannel, "Microsoft Is Making a Big Name For Itself in Acquisition Game," *Wall Street Journal,*

January 10, 2000, wsj.com; Tom Peters, *Circle of Innovation*, (New York: Knopf, 1997); www.microsoft.com; Compustat through FAME's Information Services; SmartMoney; Microsoft's MoneyCentral.

Chapter Two

1 Joe Bousquin, " 'Know What You Own' Takes On New Meaning for Peter Lynch," TheStreet.com, September 24, 1999.
2 An alternative version would distinguish internal and external relationships. Internal in this case refers to a company's workforce, or human capital, while external relationships involve customers and the supply chain.
3 Sources for material on The Williams Companies include: Gary McWilliams, "A Real Gusher in the Pipeline," *Business Week*, April 6, 1998, p. 97; "Pumping Information Through Gas Pipelines," *Business Week*, May 27, 1985, p. 142; The Williams Company, Inc., 1997 Annual Report; www.williams.com; www.hoovers.com; Compustat through FAME's Information Service; SmartMoney; and Microsoft's MoneyCentral.
4 Sources for material on General Electric include: Suzanne C. Francis, Robert H. Schaffer & Associates, "Making the Deal Real," *Harvard Business Review*, January-February 1998, p. 165; John Curran, Bethany McClean, Lixandra Urresta, "GE Capital: Jack Welch's Secret Weapon," *Fortune*, November 10, 1997, p. 116.; www.hoovers.com and www.ge.com; Compustat through FAME's Information Service; SmartMoney; and Microsoft's MoneyCentral.
5 Sources of material on Starbucks Corporation include: Howard Schultz with Dori Jones Yang, *Pour Your Heart into It*, (New York: Hyperion, 1997); www.hoovers.com; www.starbucks.com; Compustat through FAME's Information Service; SmartMoney; and Microsoft's MoneyCentral.
6 Sources for material on The Charles Schwab Corporation include: Linda Himelstein and Leah Nathans Spiro, "Schwab's New Net Message," *Business Week*, January 11, 1999, p. 49; Melanie Warner, Daniel Roth, Marc Gunther, and Erick Schonfeld, "10 Companies That Get It," *Fortune*, November 8, 1999, p. 115; Joseph Weber, "The No-Name That's Shadowing Schwab," *Business Week*, October 18, 1999, p. 184; "Schwab Profit Rises, Trading Decreases," *The New York Times*, October 15, 1999, P. 8; "Traders Drive Up Shares of Autobytel on First Day," *Austin American-Statesman*, March 27, 1999, p. G1; "Clicks and Mortar," *Chain Store Age*, September 1, 1999, p. 172; www.schwab.com; Compustate through FAME's Information Services; SmartMoney; Microsoft's MoneyCentral.
7 Sources of material on idealab! include: Bill Gross, "The New Math of Ownership," *Harvard Business Review*, November-December 1998, p. 68; www.hoovers.com.

Chapter Three

1 Carl Sagan, *The Dragons of Eden* (New York: Ballantine Books, 1977).
2 Sources for material on Egghead, Inc. include: Nikhil Hutheesing, "Last Chance for a Software Vendor," *Forbes*, June 15, 1998, p. 130; Jeanne Lee, "Egghead Averts Annihilation," *Fortune*, August 17, 1998, p. 194; www.hoovers.com.
3 "The Road to Riches," *The Economist*, January 1, 2000, p. 10-11.
4 R.H. Campbell, and R.G. Wilson, *Entrepreneurship in Britain 1750 to 1939—Documents in Economic History* (London: Adam & Charles Black, 1975), pp. 12-50.
5 There are many versions of diagrams showing economic and technological eras. See, for example: Bryan Bunch and Alexander Hellemans, *Timetables of Technology: A Chronology of the Most Important People and Events in the History of Technology* (A Touchstone Book, Simon & Schuster, Inc. 1993).
6 James W. Michaels, "How New is the New Economy?" *Forbes*, October 11, 1999, p. 47.
7 Sources of material for Sara Lee Corporation include: "Sara Lee Corporation Announces Major $1.6 Billion Restructuring Program," The Sara Lee Corporation, press release, September 15, 1997; "Sara Lee Corporation's 58th Annual Meeting of Stockholders Focuses On New Horizontal Model for Business," *Business Wire*, October 29, 1998; Sara Lee Corporation, 1998 Annual Report; www.hoovers.com; Compustat through FAME's Information Service; SmartMoney; and

Microsoft's MoneyCentral.

8 Sources of material on The Coca-Cola Company include: Betsy Morris and Patricia Sellers, "What really happened at Coke?" *Fortune,* January 17, 2000, p. 114-116; Betsy McKay and Joann S. Lublin, "Behind Coke's Massive Cuts: An Impatient Board of Directors," *Wall Street Journal,* Interactive Edition, January 27, 2000; www.hoovers.com; www.cocacola.com; Compustat through FAME's Information Service; SmartMoney; and Microsoft's MoneyCentral.

9 Betsy Morris and Patricia Sellers, "What really happened at Coke?" *Fortune,* January 17, 2000, p. 115-116.

10 Sources of information on PepsiCo Inc. include: Roger A. Enrico, "Chairman's Letter," PepsiCo, Inc., 1997 Annual Report; Compustat through FAME's Information Service; SmartMoney; and Microsoft's MoneyCentral.

11 Bernard Wysocki, Jr., "Corporate Caveat: Dell or be Delled," *Wall Street Journal,* May 10, 1999, p. A1.

12 Sources of information on Simon Property Group include: Barbara Martinez, "Simon Property to Sell Net Services to Link its Shopping-Mall Tenants," *Wall Street Journal,* November 5, 1999, p. 1.; www.simon.com; Compustat through FAME's Information Service; SmartMoney; and Microsoft's MoneyCentral.

13 Simon Property's Investor relations group (http://www.simon.com/company) reports a December 31, 1999 market capitalization of $17 billion, rather than the $4.1 billion used in our charts. The difference is Simon's umbrella partner interests.

14 Geoffrey Colvin, "How to be a Great E-CEO," *Fortune,* May 24, 1999, p 104.

Chapter Four

1 "Winning in Online Commerce Means Mastering 'Clicks and Mortar,' Says Schwab Co-CEO," PR Newswire, July 19, 1999; "Clicks and Mortar," *Chain Store Age,* September 1, 1999, p. 172.

2 Sources for material on Wal-Mart Stores, Inc. include: Barnaby J. Feder, "Dining Out at the Discount Store," *New York Times,* August 16, 1993, p. D1; Diane Frank, "The New ROI in Point of Sale," *Datamation,* November 1997, p. 73; Richard C. Halverson, "Wal-Mart to Get 100 McDonald's Units," *Discount Store News,* July 5, 1993, p. 1; Jim Lovel, "Wal-Mart, Alltel Set Price Records," Business Dateline, *Arkansas Business,* March 1, 1999, p. 27; Scott Meyer, "Full Steam Ahead for Wal-Mart," *Business and Industry,* March 8, 1999, p. 1; Kari K. Ridge and Richard Danielson, "Hungry Shoppers Can Get Big Macs at Two Wal-Marts," *St. Petersburg Times,* May 24, 1996, p. 1B; McDonald's Corporation, 1997 Annual Report; Bob Quick, "Wal Mart Gears Up for Opening," *Sante Fe New Mexican,* January 23, 1999, p. B1; "USA Company; Wal Mart Targets In-Store Logistics," EIU Views Wire, October 23, 1998; Compustat through FAME's Information Service; SmartMoney; and Microsoft's MoneyCentral.

3 "Winning in Online Commerce Means Mastering 'Clicks and Mortar,' Says Schwab Co-CEO," PR Newswire, July 19, 1999; "Clicks and Mortar," *Chain Store Age,* September 1, 1999, p. 172.

4 Sources for material on The Walt Disney Company: Bill Capodagli and Lynn Jackson, *The Disney Way* (New York: McGraw-Hill, 1999), pg. 41; Michael Iachetta, "35th Anniversary Year, Disneyland, the Original, Gets More Magical Each Day," *Chicago Tribune,* January 21, 1990, p. 21; www.hoovers.com; Compustat through FAME's Information Service; SmartMoney; and Microsoft's MoneyCentral.

5 Sources for material on Southwest Airlines include: Kevin Freiberg and Jackie Frieberg, *Nuts!* (Austin, Texas: Bard Press, 1996); www.hoovers.com; www.southwest.com; Compustat through FAME's Information Service; SmartMoney; and Microsoft's MoneyCentral.

Chapter Five

1 Po Bronson, *The First $20 Million is Always the Hardest* (New York: Random House, 1997).

2 Sources for material on Monsanto Company include: Richard A. Melcher, "Monsanto May be Counting its Chickens," *Business Week,* November 30, 1998, p. 40; Ron Stidghill, "How G.D. Searle got off its Sickbed," *Business Week,* February 24, 1997, p. 134; Ron Stodghill, "So Shall Monsanto Reap?" *Business Week,* April 1, 1996, p. 66; Julia Flynn Siler, John Carey, "Is Monsanto Burning Money in its Biotech Barn?," *Business Week,* September 2, 1991, p. 74; Thomas Jaffe, "How do you

Top This?," *Forbes,* June 1, 1998, p. 46; Thomas Jaffe, "Deal-A-Day Bob," Forbes, March 9, 1998, p. 46; Robert Lenzner, Bruce Upbin, "Monsanto v. Malthus," *Forbes,* March 10, 1997, p. 58; Linda Grant, Alicia Hills Moore, "Monsanto's Bet: There's Gold in Going Green," *Fortune,* April 14, 1997, p. 116; Joan Margretta, "Growth through Global Sustainability," *Harvard Business Review,* January-February 1997, p. 78; "Monsanto's Smarter Products," *Harvard Business Review,* January-February 1997, p. 80; "Drug Industry," *The Economist,* October 17, 1998, p. 69; www.monsanto.com; Speeches of Robert Shapiro, CEO Monsanto Company: State of the World Forum, San Francisco, CA, October, 27, 1998; Tidewater Development Conference, Washington, D.C., June 29, 1998; Biotechnology Industry Organization, New York, NY, June 17, 1998; Micro-credit Conference, New York, NY, June 27, 1998.www.hoovers.com; Compustat through FAME's Information Service; SmartMoney; and Microsoft's MoneyCentral.

3 Roger A. Enrico, "Chairman's Letter," PepsiCo, Inc., 1997 Annual Report.

4 Nikhil Deogun and Kara Scannel, "Microsoft Is Making a Big Name For Itself in Acquisition Game, *Wall Street Journal,* January 10, 2000, www.wsj.com.

5 Sources for material on Lucent Technologies Inc. include: Edward Cone, "Capricious Internet Economy Has Many Surprises for us All", *News & Record,* Greensboro, North Carolina, September 30, 1999 P. A11; George Donnelly, "Acquiring Minds," *CFO,* September 1, 1999, p. 54; Kerry Hall, "Lucent—New Company Leads the Pack," *News & Record,* Greensboro, North Carolina, May 16, 1999, p. 6; Anne Mizzi, "Lucent Cuts Legal Panel," *The Lawyer,* August 23, 1999, p. 2.; Wolfgang Saxon, "William B. Shockley, 79, Creator Of Transistor and Theory on Race," New York Times, August 14, 1989, p. 9; Da Schenoya, "Taking Stock," *Chain Store Age Executive,* October 1, 1999, p. 172; Kathy Williams and James Hart, "Don Peterson—Powering Lucent's CFO revolution," *Strategic Finance,* May 1, 1999, p. 32; "Communication Breakdown?", *Data Communications,* October 7, 1999; "AT&T Announces Plan To Split Apart; Breakup Would Be Largest Ever in U.S.," *Facts on File World News Digest,* September 28, 1995, p. 713; www.hoovers.com; Compustat through FAME's Information Service; SmartMoney; and Microsoft's MoneyCentral.

6 Sources for material on Amazon.com, Inc., include: Edward Cone, "Capricious Internet Economy Has Many Surprises for us All," *News & Record,* Greensboro, North Carolina, September 30, 1999, p. A11; Da Schenoya, "Taking Stock," *Chain Store Age* Executive with *Shopping Center Age,* October 1, 1999, p. 172; Compustat through FAME's Information Service; SmartMoney; and Microsoft's MoneyCentral.

7 Sources for the material on Cisco Systems, Inc. include: James Carbone, "Reducing Costs is a Way of Life in Electronics," *Purchasing,* May 1, 1997, p. 47; John A. Byrne, "The Corporation of the Future," *Business Week,* August 31, 1998, p. 102; Stephen Baker, Gary McWilliams, Manjeet Kripalani, "The Global Search for Brain Power;," *Business Week,* August 4, 1997, p. 46; Andy Reinhardt, Peter Burrows, Amy Barrett, "Cisco Crunch Time for a High Tech Wiz," *Business Week,* April 28, 1997, Mary Beth Grover, "Wired," *Forbes,* December 28, 1998, p. 122; Geoff Baum, "Cisco's CEO; John Chambers," *Forbes,* February 23, 1998, p. 52; Scott Woolley, "Dial Tones? No, Web Tones," *Forbes,* January 26, 1998, p. 84; Nikhil Hutheesing and Jeffery Young, "Curse of the Market Leader," *Forbes,* July 29, 1996, p. 78; Jodi Mardesich, "Cisco's Plan to Pop Up in Your Home;," Fortune, February 1, 1999, p. 119; Andrew Kuper, "The Real King of the Internet," *Fortune,* September 7, 1998, p. 84; Shawn Tully, "How Cisco Mastered the Net," *Fortune,* August, 17, 1998, p. 207; Patricia Nakache, "Cisco's Recruiting Edge," *Fortune,* August 17, 1998, p. 207; Brent Schlender, "Computing"s Next Superpower," *Fortune,* May 12, 1997, p. 88; Anne Tersesen, "Making Stay-at-Homes Feel Welcome," *Business Week,* October 12, 1998, p. 155; Compustat through FAME's Information Service; SmartMoney; and Microsoft's MoneyCentral.

Chapter Six

1 Sumantra Ghoshal and Christopher A. Bartlett, *The Individualized Corporation* (Boston: Harvard Business School Press, 1997), p. 69.

2 Sources of material on USAA include: Fred Wiersema, editor, *Customer Service,* (New York: HarperBusiness, 1998); www.hoovers.com.

3 Sources of material on DaimlerChrysler Inc. include: Joann Muller, "How Daimler Crosses the

Pond," *Business Week,* January 25, 1999, p. 6; www.hoovers.com; Charles Fine, *Clockspeed* (Cambridge, Massachusetts: Perseus, 1998); www.daimlerchrysler.com.

4 "Then Came Branson," *Business Week* (int'l edition), October 26, 1998, p. 116.

5 Ibid., p. 116.

6 Additional sources for material on Virgin Group, Ltd., include: *Financial Times,* London, December 24, 1998, p. 10; *The Guardian,* London, October 11, 1999, p. 20; www.hoovers.com; www.virgin.com.

7 Sources of material on Psion include: Jean Max, Peggy Salz-Troutman, Charles Wallace, "Psion of the Times," *Time,* November 23, 1998, p. 46; Anil Bhoyrul and James Hipwell, "City Slickers", *The Mirror,* October 6, 1999, p. 32; Terho Uimonen, "Swedish Bank in Big Wireless App Test," *Computerworld,* October 11, 1999, p. 25; www.hoovers.com.

Chapter Seven

1 B. Joseph Pine, Don Peppers and Martha Rogers, "Do You Want to Keep Your Customers Forever?," *Harvard Business Review,* March-April 1995, p. 103.

2 Jeffery Laderman, "Remaking Schwab," *Business Week,* May 25, 1998, p. 122.

3 Sources of material relating to AlliedSignal, Inc. include: Lawrence A. Bossidy, "Reality-Based Leadership," speech, delivered to The Economic Club of Washington, D.C., June 16, 1996; Anthony L. Velocci, Jr., "Merger Pact Requires Avionics Divestitures," *Aviation Week and Space Technology,* October 11, 1999, p. 93.

4 Source: www.gillette.com (Investors: Business and Investment); www.duracell.com.

5 Sources for material on Autobytel.com, Inc. include: Johnathan Rosenoer, Douglas Armstrong, J.Russell Gates, *The Clickable Corporation* (New York: Free Press, 1999); John Couretas, "Despite Losses, Autobytel.com Plans to Woo Wall St. Investors," *Automotive News,* February 1, 1999, p. 18; Jonathan Gaw, "Million-Dollar Claim Revs Up Autobytel Stock," *Los Angeles Times,* May 28, 1999, p. 1; Chris Knap, "Autobytel IPO pulls in with $103.5 million," *The Orange County Register,* March 27, 1999, p. C01; David Welch, "Buying a Car by Computer—The Internet is taking Over How You Can Purchase An Auto," *Asheville Citizen-Times,* Asheville, North Carolina, March 30, 1999, p. C1.; "Autobytel Drives Car Shoppers through the Internet," *Bank Technology News,* October, 1998; www.hoovers.com; www.autobytel.com; Compustat through FAME's Information Service; SmartMoney; and Microsoft's MoneyCentral.

Chapter Eight

1 R.H. Campbell and R.G.Wilson, *Entrepreneurship in Britain 1750—1939, Documents in Economic History* (Adam & Charles Black, London 1975), p. 21.

2 David Lamb, "Schwarzkopf Tries Not To Wear Out Hero's Welcome," *Los Angeles Times,* October 20, 1991, p. A1.

3 Sources for the material on Apple Computer, Inc. include: Michael Krantz, "What Flavor is Your Mac?," *Time,* January 18, 1999, p. 92; "A Boss's Life," *Business Week,* January 11, 1999, p. 63; Philip Elmer-Dewitt, "Steve Jobs: Apple's Anti-Gates," *Time,* December 7, 1998, p.205; Joan C. O'Hamilton, "At Long Last, Apple Gets it Right," *Business Week,* November 16, 1998, p. 154; Stephen H. Wildstrom, "Is iMac for You?," *Business Week,* September 7, 1998, p. 18; "Steve Jobs: There's Sanity Returning," *Business Week,* May 25, 1998, p. 62; Ira Sager, Peter Burrows, Andy Reinhardt, "Back to the Future at Apple," *Business Week,* May 25, 1998, p. 56.; Compustat through FAME's Information Service; SmartMoney; and Microsoft's MoneyCentral.

4 Steve Lohr, "Big Blue Casts Itself as Big Brother to Business on the Web," *New York Times,* September 22, 1999, section G, p. 50. Other sources of information on IBM include Compustat through FAME's Information Service; SmartMoney; and Microsoft's MoneyCentral.

5 Lou Gerstner, speech delivered to the 1997 IBM Annual Meeting of Stockholders, Dallas, Texas, April 29, 1997.

6 Sources for material on Johnson & Johnson include: Brian O'Reilly and Ronald B. Lieber, "J&J in on a Roll," *Fortune,* December 26, 1994, p. 178; www.jnj.com; Compustat through FAME's Information Service; SmartMoney; and Microsoft's MoneyCentral.

7 Michael Hammer, *Beyond Reengineering* (New York: Harper Collins, 1996), p. 191.

8 Sources for material on Pfizer, Inc. include: "Earnings Roundup—Drug Firms' Profits Rise on Strong Sales," *Los Angeles Times*, October 20, 1999, p. 3; Scott Woolley, "Science & Savy," *Forbes*, January 11, 1999, p. 122; www.pfizer.com; Compustat through FAME's Information Service; SmartMoney; and Microsoft's MoneyCentral.

9 Sources for material on The Procter & Gamble Company include: Steve Matthews, "Procter & Gamble Shuffle Cuts 15,000 Jobs—Consumer Firm Puts Focus on New Products," *Chattanooga Times / Chattanooga Free Press*, June 10, 1999, p. C1; www.pg.com; Compustat through FAME's Information Service; SmartMoney; and Microsoft's MoneyCentral.

10 See also, John Grant, *The New Marketing Manifesto—The 12 Rules for Building Successful Brands in the 21st Century* (Orion Business Books, 1999).

11 Xerox Corporation, 1997 Annual Report; Max Jarman, "Xerox Alters Name, Recaptures Business," *The Arizona Republic*, February 7, 1999, p. D4; www.xerox.com.

Chapter Nine

1 Sources for the material on Newell Rubbermaid, Inc. include: Cynthia A Montgomery, "Creating Corporate Advantage," *Harvard Business Review*, May-June, 1998, p.71; "Newell-Rubbermaid Merger to Create Powerhouse," *Chain Drug Review*, January 18, 1999, p. 59; "Newell to Acquire Rubbermaid for 27.0 Times Earnings," *Corporate Growth Report*, October 26, 1998, p. 9848; www.newell-rubbermaid.com; Compustat through FAME's Information Service; SmartMoney; and Microsoft's MoneyCentral.

Chapter Ten

1 CNBC, on-line video report, July 19, 1999.

2 "No Charge", *US Airways Attache*, September 1999, p. 15.

3 Simon Avery, "Free PC Offer Brings in 500,000 Applications," *National Post*, February 11, 1999, p. C11; "No Charge," *US Airways Attache*, September 1999, p. 16.

4 www.britannica.com.

5 Jon G. Auerbach, "IBM Sees Internet Playing Big Role in its Future," *Wall Street Journal*, May 13, 1999, p. B9.

6 David Kline, "Discovering New Value in Intellectual Property," *Harvard Business Review*, January-February 2000.

7 Sources of material on CMGI, Inc. include: "Web Handicapper CMG Places a Big Bet on Genealogy," by Jon G. Auerbach, *Wall Street Journal*, December 17, 1998; Dennis Callaghan, "CMGI's Excellent £Venture," *MC Technology Marketing Intelligence*, August 1, 1999, p. 22; Dennis Callaghan, "Ancestry.com, Inc.," *Adweek*, Eastern edition, October 4, 1999, p. 62; Diane Mermigas, "CMGI'S Wetherell Playing By His Own Rules," *Electronic Media*, May 17, 1999, p. 22; Compustat through FAME's Information Service; SmartMoney; and Microsoft's MoneyCentral.

8 Sources for material on British Airways, plc include: Helen Gibson, Bruce Crumley, "Europe's Flexible Flyers," *Time*, September, 7, 1998, p. 53; "British Airways Reporting its First Quarterly Loss in Nearly Four Years," *Aviation Week and Space Technology*, February 15, 1999, p. 19; Adam Woods, "*British Airways*," *Precision Marketing*, October 12, 1998, p. 31; Lucy Killgren, "Flying Colours;," *Marketing Week*, July 23, 1998, p. 25; 1998 Annual Report; Sir Colin Marshall, "Letter to Shareholders," www.british-airways.com.

Chapter Eleven

1 Peter L. Bernstein, *Against the Gods—The Remarkable Story of Risk* (New York: John Wiley & Sons, Inc., 1996), p. 1.

2 Shawn Tully, Tim Carvell, "So Mr. Bossidy, We Know You can Cut," *Fortune*, August 21, 1995, p. 70.

3 Andrew Grove, *Only the Paranoid Survive* (New York: Currency Book/Doubleday, 1996).

4 Charles Gasparino and Rebecca Buckman, "Facing Internet Threat, Merrill to Offer Trading Online for Low Fees," *Wall Street Journal*, June 1, 1999, p. 1.

5 Ibid., p. 1.

6 Sources of material on Gillette Company include: Jeremy Kahn, "Gillette Loses Face," *Fortune*, November 8, 1999, p. 147; "Mergers and Acquisitions—Gillette to Buy Duracell," Facts on File, *World News Digest*, September 19, 1996, p. 681; "No Charge", *US Airways Attache*, September 1999; SmartMoney.

7 Sources of material on Chase Manhattan Bank include: Timothy O'Brien, "Market Place—Taking the Danger Out of Risk," *New York Times*, January 20, 1999, p. C1; "Chase's Growth Tied to Info-Based Marketing," *American Banker Financial Services Marketing Supplement*, Winter 1998, pp. 1a, 6a-8a.

8 Donald L. Boudreau, "Keynote Address," speech, delivered at the Best Practices in Retail Banking Symposium, Phoenix, A.Z., February 25, 1998.

Chapter Twelve

1 Sources for material on LinkExchange, Inc. include: www.hoovers.com; www.linkexchange.com, which is now www.bcentral.com

2 Sources for material on Calyx & Corolla, Inc., include: Steve Jordon, "Idea Germinates Custom Service For Fresh Flowers," *Omaha World Herald*, May 4, 1996, p. 56; Michael Leach, "Deal Brings Sweet Smell of Success for Cut Flower Catalog," *The Columbus Dispatch*, May 21, 1994, p. 2C; Ellen Neuborne, "Catalog Growth Stems from Personal Touch", *USA Today*, May 10, 1993, p. 5E; "Entrepreneur Profile: Ruth Owades," *San Francisco Business Times*, December 11, 1998, p. 29.

3 Sources of material on FDX Corporation include: Jay Palmer, "Three, Two, One . . .," *Barrons Online*, December 7, 1998; www.fdxcorp.com.

4 Sources for the material on Mary Kay, Inc. include: "Mary Kay's New Venture," *WWD*, February 19, 1999, p. 8; Kathryn T. Curt and William L. Shanklin, "The Wall: How Mary Kay Cosmetics Knocks it Down," *Marketing Management*, Fall/Winter 1998, p. 42; Laura Klepack, "Mary Kay; Mary Kay Inc.," *WWD*, September 28, 1998, p. 2105; www.hoovers.com.

5 Sources for material on Priceline.com include: Matthew Lubanko, "Empty Pocket But Stock A Rocket," *The Hartford Courant*, May 5, 1999, p. D1; SmartMoney.

Chapter Thirteen

1 Peter Drucker, "The Next Information Revolution," *Forbes* ASAP, August 24, 1998, p. 46.

2 William Gates, III, *"Business @ The Speed of Thought: Using a Digital Nervous System,"* (Warner Books, Inc., New York, 1999).

3 Bear, Stearns & Co. analysis.

4 "The Patent & License Exchange Inc. Woos Wedbush Morgan Medical Tech Analyst," *Business Wire*—September 28, 1999.

5 www.mediametrix.com.

6 Leif Edvinsson and Michael S. Malone, *Intellectual Capital: Realizing Your Company's True Value by Finding Its Hidden Brainpower,* New York; (HarperBusiness, 1997), p. 21.

7 Christopher Shilakes and Julie Tylman, Enterprise Information Portals—Move over Yahoo! Merrill Lynch & Co., November 16, 1998.

8 Stephen Barr, *CFO* Magazine, September 1999

9 Robert Simons, *Levers of Control,* (Harvard Business School Press: Bost, MA, 1995).

10 Steven M.H. Wallman, Senior Fellow, The Brookings Institution, "The Impact of the Internet on the Future of Financial Reporting," speech delivered January 18, 2000.

11 Gregory L. White, "E-ssembly Lines: How GM, Ford Think Web Can Make a Splash On the Factory Floor By Forcing Suppliers Online, Car Makers May Ignite New Internet Sales Boom," *Wall Street Journal*, December 3, 1999, www.wsj.com.

12 Ibid, www.wsj.com.

INDEX

About the Authors

Richard Boulton is Arthur Andersen's worldwide managing partner for strategy and planning, with offices in London and Chicago. He is responsible for the firm's global service offerings (assurance, tax, consulting and corporate finance) and Web-based knowledge businesses. He is the author of a number of published articles on the valuation and exploitation of intellectual property. Richard joined Arthur Andersen in London in 1981 after graduating from Oriel College, Oxford University. He lives in Woking, England with his wife, Fiona, and his two children, Honor and Fraser.

Barry Libert, who joined Arthur Andersen as a partner in 1995, is a worldwide lecturer and consultant on value creation and its impact on business models, corporate investment, and technology strategies in the New Economy. After earning a Masters of Business Administration from Columbia Business School, he joined McKinsey & Company as a management consultant and later served as managing director of Hancock Realty Investors. He also established and sold a number of successful enterprises. Barry lives in Boston with his wife, Ellen, and two sons, Michael and Adam.

Steve Samek, managing partner of Arthur Andersen's U.S. operations, is responsible for more than 25,000 professionals located in offices throughout the country. He joined Arthur Andersen 26 years ago. During his tenure, Steve has held a series of leadership positions and today sits on the firm's Board of Partners. He is the co-author of several books on strategy development. He now resides in Wheaton, Illinois with his wife, Linda, and their four children, Adam, Scott, Hillary and Brittany.

About Arthur Andersen

Arthur Andersen's new strategy embraces historic shifts in the economy; focuses on the growing importance of intangible assets; and positions the organization to help clients create, manage and measure value in the New Economy. With world-class skills in assurance, tax, consulting and corporate finance, Arthur Andersen has more than 77,000 people in over 84 countries who are united by a single worldwide operating structure that fosters inventiveness, knowledge sharing and a focus on client success. Since its beginning in 1913, Arthur Andersen has realized 86 years of uninterrupted growth.